Advance Praise for:

YOU

CAN

AFFORD TO DIE

Sensible Advice From a Practical Funeral Director

"With a unique combination of compassion and candor, Joe Kalmer offers valuable information that every person needs in order to provide real security for their family. After reading this book, I have a completely different view of funeral planning, which now seems as 'de-mystified' as insuring my home, or any other much needed service I would consider. Thank you Joe, for making a complex topic both easy *and* comfortable to understand."

~ Adrianna Larkin, radio host of
Sacred Fire Living and author of
*Igniting the Sacred Fire,
Reinventing Yourself at Any Age*

"About thirty years ago the Pletcher Funeral Home doorbell rang. When I answered it, I met a young man who was a student at SIUE. He was inquiring about part-time work, and what an impression he made! That was the beginning of my relationship with Joe Kalmer. Upon his graduation from Worsham College of Mortuary Science, I offered him a job as a funeral director. He was a hard worker and was always willing to help people in any way. This book will help people (again) by providing them the knowledge for making wise decisions when planning a funeral."

~ Dean Pletcher, Former Owner,
Pletcher Funeral Home, Edwardsville, Illinois

"As someone who is still in the 'sandwich zone' of paying off student loans from the kids' college and planning care for aging parents, I really appreciate this information. It's an easy informative read that is chock full of information. More importantly, it's common sense advice written for the everyday guy. Thanks Joe."

~ Mike Herold, owner of
Handyman Herold

"This book offers an insight into a subject that no one wants to discuss – death. Joe takes this subject and puts it into terms that we can all relate to. He breaks it down to palatable options and helps you take it one step at a time. Sometime in their life, everyone will have to deal with this topic. Thank you, Joe, for helping everyone have a better understanding…"

~Dawn Mushill, author of
Customer Service and Beyond

"Funerals are not a fun topic, but even worse is being taken advantage of at a time when you are most vulnerable. Joe's book does a great job of explaining the process much like you would have a conversation with a close friend. You can really tell how much he wants to help you get through the process with as little pain as possible. I highly recommend this book to anyone who wants to be prepared and coached by not only an expert, but by someone who cares about you and your family."

~Danelle Brown,
Business Coach and Author of
*Soulmate Proprietors: How To
Run A Business With Your
Spouse and STAY Married!*

YOU

CAN

AFFORD TO DIE

Sensible Advice From a Practical
Funeral Director

KMS

Publishing

Published by KMS Publishing

This publication was created with the intent of providing accurate
and authoritative information in regard to the subject matter
covered. It is designed as a guide with the express understanding
that laws can vary from state to state regarding disposition of the
deceased and are subject to change at any time. If information is
received that contradicts what is enclosed, the services of a
competent legal professional should be sought.

Cover design by Lauren Stewart
Cover photography licensed from Dreamstime.com
Photographer: Ken Cole
Edited by Gloria Horrell & Minan Publishing

First edition printed in the United States of America

ISBN: 978-0-9831726-0-4

For permission to use selections from this book contact:

KMS Publishing,
8638 US Hwy 50,
Lebanon, IL 62254

In Memory of Gloria Horrell

Table of Contents

Foreword xi

Acknowledgements xix

Introduction 1

Chapter 1: The Need for Trust 7

Chapter 2: Image 13

Chapter 3: Vulnerability 23

Chapter 4: Federal Intervention 33

Chapter 5: Let's Go Shopping 41

Chapter 6: Goods and Services 47

Chapter 7: Merchandise (Caskets) 65

Chapter 8: Merchandise (Vaults) 73

Chapter 9: Clothing and Flowers 81

Chapter 10: Urns 87

Chapter 11: Cash Advances 91

Chapter 12: Pre-Need 101

Chapter 13: I Love Cremation 115

Chapter 14: Making a Change 122

Chapter 15: Just What I Need 131

Chapter 16: Will You Join Me? 141

Chapter 17: Conclusion 149

Appendix 159

    Funeral Planning Checklist 161

    Exhibit A: Cost Analysis of a Traditional Funeral 167

    Exhibit B: Option 1, Cost Reduction 173

    Exhibit C: Option 2, Cost Reduction 179

    Exhibit D: Option 3, Cost Reduction 185

Foreword

"Show me the manner in which a nation or community cares for its dead, and I will measure with mathematical exactness, the tender mercies of its people, their respect for the laws of the land, and their loyalties to high ideals."
~Sir William Gladstone

I've known Joe Kalmer his entire professional life. He enrolled in Mortuary School in 1987 and came to live in the funeral home where I was employed. In the Chicago area, some funeral homes house students while they are enrolled in mortuary school. They receive a room or an apartment in which to live and a salary, often meager, but an income nonetheless. In exchange, the mortuary student assists the funeral home staff with any task that may be assigned to him, usually mundane or cumbersome ones that licensed funeral directors don't wish to do, and don't have to do, because they have a student. Mortuary students are at the very bottom of the funeral home hierarchy.

Joe was different from prior students. He was a quick study and he understood how the game was played: sort of a dues paying or rite of passage. After all, we all basically know how to do laundry, mop floors and wash cars! This new mortuary student we had stumbled upon not only handled the tasks given to him, but wanted more. In a very short time after his arrival, Joe had mastered the basic tasks and was moving on to handling phone calls, assisting at visitations and funerals, and removing remains from their respective places of death. When a first call came in to the funeral home fifteen minutes before it was time to go home for the day, Joe was one of the first to grab his jacket and ask, "Where are we headed?" Joe was different. Joe cared about people, was of high moral character, and wanted to learn as much as he could about Funeral Service while he lived and worked with us.

Although I don't actually remember having the discussion with him, funeral directors inevitably ask each other in idle conversation the question, "Why?" Why does one choose this as a career? Is it because you have a calling to help people through some of the saddest and most difficult times of their lives? Is it because you enjoy the fact that no two days are ever the same—as they would be if you sat in the same cubicle in an office building day after day? Or is it because a substantial investment of capital, coupled with good old fashioned hard work, might generate enough profit to provide a decent living for your family? I think Joe would have answered these questions like he answers all questions: honestly, with a hint of a twinkle in his eye…and "YES!"

After his graduation, Joe went home to serve an apprenticeship in Edwardsville, Illinois. Upon completing that, he obtained his Funeral Director/Embalmer license and continued to work at that same funeral home--which he eventually ended up purchasing. After owning his own funeral home for a number of years which included a complete remodeling, Joe sold the funeral home to another firm in his town. He was employed by that firm, and was happy there, but eventually Joe came to the conclusion again that it was time for a change and moved on from there to begin his newest business venture, "Kalmer Memorial Services" in O'Fallon, Illinois.

Change is an essential element of success in anyone's career, or for that matter in the success of any business. Funeral Service is no different—there have been many changes since the ancient Egyptians began to mummify the dead. They believed that the body must be preserved so that the spirit might inhabit it again someday. During the next 1,500 years or so, advances were made in embalming—not specifically for burying the dead, but rather to preserve human tissue for anatomical research.

The Civil War brought great advances in Funeral Service. Embalming techniques were advanced enough to enable fallen combatants to be shipped home for burial. In all wars prior, the dead were for the most part buried on the battlefield in which they were killed. Following the Civil War, the assassination of Abraham Lincoln with his subsequent one month "funeral tour" of the country caught the attention of the general public. Embalming schools began to emerge to teach the art of embalming. Coffin companies were formed, often times from the town furniture maker, to supply families with coffins to be used to bury loved ones. Some of these furniture store/coffin manufacturers went so far as not only supplying the merchandise for a funeral, but to "undertake" the task of handling the funeral proper. These "Undertakers", as they were now called, began to build buildings for people to gather for services after the death of a loved one instead of viewing the deceased in the "parlors" of their own homes. Funeral (Parlors) Homes were born.

Arguably, the latest change that has impacted Funeral Service is the internet. The internet was in its infancy when Joe and I were in school. However, it will now allow anyone with a modem instant access to information from across the globe. Information flows at lightning speed worldwide, true or untrue, for all to see and use. It is not uncommon for family members to bring various electronic devices along with them to the funeral home when they come to make arrangements.

While it is true that the many advances have occurred throughout history regarding the science of funerals, the reasons we hold funerals for our loved ones has pretty much remained constant. Funerals are for the LIVING. Funerals provide a means of closure for the immediate family of the deceased, as well as the community at large. They celebrate a life that was lived, and allow friends and neighbors to show sympathy and support to the family at a sorrowful time. This holds true no matter what kind of funeral is arranged as well as whatever your individual belief concerning what comes next for the deceased.

I would guess that cost is probably at the top of everyone's list of concerns when it comes to funerals.

Maintaining the traditions that funerals have amassed over time can be expensive. Cemetery costs, casket, visitation, services, luncheon, flowers, etc. add up pretty fast. No one is denying the fact that funerals can be expensive, but a dignified funeral can be arranged much more economically than you might think. The key to this, in my opinion, is knowledge. The more you understand about a subject (in this case funerals) the better equipped you are to make sound decisions. In light of the circumstances in which you will be making these decisions immediately after the death of a loved one, knowledge is essential.

Knowledge can come from many sources. I think the best knowledge anyone can acquire comes from experience. You can read all of the information you can find about electricity and current and grounding and may certainly understand the concepts, but nothing brings it home to be permanently implanted in your brain as the day you come in contact with an electric fence! The same holds true for funerals: you may read all you care to read, gather all of the information you can, and still not have enough knowledge to make practical choices. On average, a person makes funeral arrangements less than six times in his or her lifetime. Hardly enough experience to be knowledgeable about the subject.

That's why a funeral director is such a great resource. He or she is a treasure trove of information regarding funeral services. They can not only arrange a meaningful funeral for your loved one, they can navigate the maze of local, county, state, and in some cases, international paperwork involved. Funeral directors, contrary to the beliefs of some, are not people who wring their hands when you enter the funeral home, ready to deplete the family resources. Granted, funeral directors are businessmen and women, but NO business shall remain in business for any length of time if they purposely force people into buying things they know they can't pay for. It's offensive and makes absolutely no sense from a business standpoint. We make a significant investment of time and money to build businesses, and more importantly, our reputations.

That's why I think this book needed to be written, and needs to be read. My friend Joe is the perfect funeral director for this endeavor. Without sounding like a commercial advertisement, he is a knowledgeable funeral service professional with years of experience. Joe has gone from mortuary student to apprentice, employee, owner, and now owner of a new business and author. He has seen many changes in funeral service and is consistently on the cutting edge of new ways of serving the families that call upon him during times of great sorrow.

It is my sincere hope that you read this book and gain some insight on what being a funeral service professional means in today's world. Feel free to be entertained a bit by Joe's laid back manner and ability to tell a story---he has a "down home" air about him that will instantly put you at ease. More importantly, learn what it takes to run a successful business in an industry in which most of the clientele are facing the most difficult times of their lives. Take the knowledge gained from reading this book and think about your personal wishes and plans before the time arises. If you take nothing else from this book remember that there are professionals like Joe on duty 24 hours per day, 7 days per week, 365 days per year who are prepared for the honor of caring for your loved one and will, "with mathematical exactness" provide your family with practical, dignified, funeral service.

~John L. Rife, Crest Hill, Illinois

Acknowledgements

To my beautiful wife and daughters Cheryl, Kelsie and Olivia: Being the wife and children of a funeral director is never easy. Your love for me and respect for what I do are what keeps me going. You make it all worthwhile.

To my Mom and Dad, Sue and Norb: Thank you for life. Being raised in a home full of love, warmth, and kindness has made be a better man.

To Aunt Rose and Uncle John, my "other-in-laws": Without your love and support, this journey would have been even more difficult. Our "Friday Night Fish Fries" will give me a lifetime of memories.

To my siblings, Carol, John, Beth, Darla and their families: Your individual victories in the face of adversities are inspiring. You make me proud to be your brother.

To Dean and Judy Pletcher: Thank you for giving me a chance way back in 1984. I am infinitely grateful for your loyalty to me and support of my decisions.

To all of my 'funeral friends' and colleagues who have offered their support and encouragement. You know who you are: I appreciate each and every one of you.

And to all my other friends and family, too numerous to mention, who have offered their advice, encouragement, sweat equity, support and prayers: Thank you, thank you, thank you.

To Dr. Michael Mulligan and Father Jeff Goeckner: Thank you for keeping me healthy--mind, body and soul.

Introduction

Thirty one.

If memory serves me correctly, that is the record: thirty one. As a young boy intimidated with the thought of leaving home the first day of kindergarten, my older sister had to think of a way to keep my mind occupied. She may have had the idea from our mother, but I don't know. Nevertheless, counting dead frogs on the streets of Germantown, Illinois from our home to our school six blocks away was worth a try — and it worked.

For whatever morbid reason, I was interested in those dead frogs. I guess in 1968, the climate was wetter and the lakes were higher. Consequently, there were lots of frogs crossing the streets, apparently inattentive to the passing cars which were about to end their wet lives. I had plenty to think about those first few days of the next phase of my young life: my first teacher, Mrs. Bohannon, my new friends, the cute girl in the next row, homework, and everything else that could fill a five-year-old's mind; yet all I thought about were those frogs.

Those *dead* frogs.

It might have been fourteen the first day, eighteen the second, and sixteen the third. After school, I would sometimes walk a different route and start the counting anew. Other times I would walk the same route and re-count. Were they still there? If not, where were they? Were they dragged off by dogs? Were there any more frog casualties? Why were some of them "picked apart"? I discovered the answer to the last question by witnessing a black crow nibbling away at one. To me, that was fascinating.

Although too young to know it, I was witnessing nature at its best. The frogs were born, they lived, they died. And if left exactly where they perished, they decomposed and were eaten by other creatures in the food chain.

In due time, I noticed a lot of death: deer on the highway, cats on the street, dogs in the ditch, squirrels fallen from a tree. If it was dead and within my sight, I noticed it. Not only did I notice it, I examined it. Not in a grotesque way; I was content in poking at it with a stick and I would never bring it home—much to the relief of my mother; but I did look at it very closely.

Introduction

We didn't have an "animal control" department in our small town, so at times, I was able to actually see the increasing level of decomposition as the days passed; faster in the summer, slower in the winter. Call it a morbid fascination, but it got my attention. I knew where all of the remains were. I would visit and revisit the site of their demise, anxiously anticipating whatever it was I was about to see. If left ignored, and satisfied that I had seen enough, I would take it upon myself to bury the carcass, giving it a "proper" burial.

In my teenage years I worked for the Youth Conservation Corps. The YCC was a group of young men and women who cleaned up our state parks, maintained campgrounds, rip-rapped ditches, built small walkway bridges, etc. When we would find a dead animal, I was the one designated to "provide for its disposition"

— and I would gladly do so.

One day, we discovered a raccoon in its later stages of decomposition, maggots and all. My coworkers were amazed I could stare at the rotting animal while eating my lunch. That was the day I discovered the strength of my stomach; an attribute which would serve me well in the future.

Thinking back on my childhood and the aforementioned interest in all things dead, it seems I could've gone wayward, off the beaten path; a path which could've lead to a more destructive lifestyle. Today it might be compared to a "gothic" interest. The truth is, I was fascinated with the whole cycle of life. Just like our canine and feline friends as well as all species: we're born, we live, we die.

I believe science and religion will never agree on much, but I feel both are necessary to be born. God creates life but lets the doctors keep mom and baby healthy. What makes us live? What makes us die?

Not long ago while driving in the country, a rabbit darted out in front of me. I swerved to miss but didn't. One minute earlier that rabbit was alive and well, living his life to the fullest and the next minute that life was extinguished, snuffed out by a combination of his nerve and my driving speed.

Introduction

I didn't go back to "examine" the rabbit, as I would have as a boy, but I did think about the days that were....and the days that are....and the days that will be....

For me, "the days that were", lead me to mortuary school. With my unique interest in death, logic would dictate that I had a high probability of being either a serial killer or a funeral director. Much to the relief of my parents, I chose the latter. It was a good fit. I wasn't taught about providing those animals with what's described as a proper burial, but it seemed like the natural thing to do.

Someone has to take it upon him or herself to dispose of the dead, whether it's man or beast; burial or cremation. People experiencing grief need honest guidance, and professional yet compassionate service. Being a funeral director is a sort of calling, I suppose. Yet even those of us who do it with the greatest amount of heart and integrity understand: it still has to be handled as a "business", otherwise the "service" cannot continue.

For me, it all started with those first intimidating days of my elementary education. "Let's count the dead frogs, Joey." Indeed I did, Beth. And I'm still counting. When I go back to Germantown, Illinois to visit my mother, now widowed and candidly talking to me about her own demise, I traverse those same streets but don't see the frogs anymore. They're still dead. They're just dead somewhere else.

I guess the record of thirty one will forever stand.

Chapter 1

The Need For Trust

Statistics tell us that in our lifetime we will probably make funeral arrangements three times. It may be for our mother, father, grandmother, aunt, uncle, close friend, or, God forbid, a child. I have already been on that side of the desk three times, and I'm only 47 — so maybe those statistics are conservative. Or perhaps I'm simply not random enough or live slightly beyond the norm.

As it is, my family gets off the hook easily when these times arise. As a funeral director, I know what we need, how to get it, whom to contact, how many death certificates we'll need, and the list goes on...that seemingly endless and bewildering list that involves Social Security, the VA, insurance companies, and any number of "incidentals" that need to be dealt with after someone dies.

When my father died in 2007, I drove the 40 miles to his home so I could *do the removal* and take him back to my funeral home where he would be embalmed. On my way back, I thought about all of the times I had done exactly that from another family's home, and they didn't even know me. I was a stranger…but there I was, putting *their* father in the back of my van and driving off.

It was then I realized just how important a director's job is and what a great amount of trust needs to be established in such a short period of time. I was honored I could do that for my dad—as I'm continually honored by providing the care entrusted to me by our clients. But I also thought about those families who don't know their funeral director, and I add my hope to theirs that the director that they choose will guide them appropriately and honestly.

I'd like to think they would, but as in any other business or profession, we have our bad apples. In the old days, I knew of funeral homes with two price lists, one for most people and the other for those who could afford more—obviously neither appropriate nor honest. And although that doesn't happen anymore, there are always real or imagined issues, just or unjust complaints. It goes with the territory during emotional times.

I am always asked about the average cost of a funeral, which, in one sense is much like asking, "What's the average price of a car?" Just like cars, there are many types of funerals, but not every death will result in one. You have many choices: traditional funeral with a burial, cremation with a viewing, cremation without a viewing but with a service, direct cremation or "immediate" cremation with no service, anatomical donation, immediate burial and graveside service — just to name a few.

We can even add "green burial" to the list, the eco-friendly way to bury the dead: no embalming, a simple all wood casket or perhaps a gunny sack (literally, if allowed) buried in a shallow grave as quickly as possible. Many see it as a giving back to nature, and take solace as flowers grow from the remains returning to the earth..."ashes to ashes, dust to dust..."

When asked about the average cost of a funeral my reply is "about a fourth of the cost of an average wedding." That's right. And while some find it acceptable to spend $50,000 on a wedding that has 52% chance of ending in divorce, spending $12,500 on a funeral for the woman who gave them life is often considered out of the question.

In brief explanation, if someone says they paid $12,000 for a funeral, the cost probably included cemetery expenses: grave space, grave opening and closing fees, temporary marker, and perpetual care—which could total $3,000 or more. Oftentimes this is incorrectly referred to as "funeral expenses," not "cemetery expenses." The consumer needs to know the difference, and that's part of my intent with this book. Just like the funeral itself, there are many choices at the cemetery. The funeral director controls none of them, other than informing the family and providing empathetic guidance in their decisions.

As a licensed funeral professional with over two decades of experience (which is nothing compared to the guys who used to embalm without gloves), I have acquired the skills necessary to embalm a body, put one back together after a traumatic death, and listen intently to those who are grieving. I have developed more compassion than I ever thought possible, become a more patient man with less of a temper, and have witnessed enough sadness that I thank God every day for simply rising from my bed.

I have learned to never take anything for granted because it could all end in an instant. Thankfully, I have learned this only in my role as a witness to life and death— not personal experience. I am truly grateful, as I acknowledge my hope every day that it stays that way.

Because I have been richly blessed, I offer this book with the intent that it will enlighten you about the funeral industry. I'll share a few stories along the way—stories which I feel will accent my point and hopefully entertain you a little. Understandably, any time I share a story about a death or a funeral there is something morbidly comical about it. If it were not, it probably wouldn't be much of a story. But mainly I intend to inform you, the consumer that you don't have to spend $12,000 on a funeral. There are ways to spend a lot less and feel like you've received just as much if not more.

It's not about being cheap. It's about being practical.

The title of this book came from a conversation I was having with a friend who bluntly told me that he couldn't even afford to die. Without the knowledge that I am going to share with you, it certainly would seem that way. You *can* afford to die...

I'll show you.

Notes

_____

_____

_____

_____

_____

_____

_____

_____

_____

_____

_____

Chapter 2

Image

The typical funeral home owner evokes an image of a prominent personality, someone who plays golf at the local country club, has dinner at the finest restaurants, is a worldly traveler, and schmooze's the public as if he or she were running for office. Friends of mine poke fun at me when we are out somewhere, even in another town, and I run into someone who knows me.

The truth is, when you are a funeral director in the same town for over 20 years, you develop relationships. These are often relationships formed at the most difficult time in a person's life...the death of a loved one. Sometimes the family doesn't know me and is meeting me for the very first time; but after three days, they know me well.

One of the nicest compliments I have ever received happened about a year ago. I was at the golf course (naturally) when an unfamiliar woman approached me and said, "Hi, how have you been? You may not remember me, but you buried my mother about 15 years ago." I was impressed with her memory, which she attributed to how well she and her family had been treated by me and my staff.

When someone speaks of a funeral director, some of the first thoughts that come to mind are big black cars, fancy suits, cuff links, designer ties, and large impressive buildings. Is that wrong? No. Because in the past, that's the way it was. Although I have colleagues who still project that image, I prefer shorts or blue jeans when I have no funerals or appointments. I never wear cuff links, I don't own my funeral cars (I rent), and I still haven't been to Europe.

If a funeral director *does* drive a Lincoln or a Cadillac, he has probably earned it. Chances are that for the past 25 years he has been putting in long hours, sacrificing family vacations, missing soccer games because of visitations, and embalming two bodies while the rest of the family enjoys Thanksgiving dinner. One of my older friends in the business always wanted a Lincoln but thought it was pretentious—so instead, he always drove a Mercury. Upon his retirement, I thought he would finally buy that Lincoln...but he didn't.

You see, my friend is not cheap. In addition to being unpretentious, he's practical. A Mercury is a very nice car and provides a professional appearance when leading a funeral procession. It's also about $15,000 less than a new Lincoln. We'll talk more about that later.

I love the funeral profession. I am proud to be a funeral director and embalmer. As much a *vocation* as a *profession,* a funeral director also serves as embalmer, car washer, and maintenance man...at times we are also minister (I can do the 23rd Psalm and the Lord's Prayer as well as any clergy), psychologist ("joy shared is joy increased; grief shared is grief diminished"), and counselor, providing guidance with difficult decisions at a most trying time. Many days are routine—but once in awhile you have a day you'll never forget. But those stories are for another book.

As much as I love the profession and most of my colleagues, I have found that many of us still brag about "the coppers" we sold last month or the mahogany casket that retails for about nine grand. Some of us still get caught up in the new Cadillac hearse we just bought at the convention or the $4000 embalming table we had to purchase at the end of our fiscal year. While those things may have their own small moment of importance to the business, my priorities are focused in a different direction.

I don't ever want to lose sight of the humble beginnings from which I came; or how my father worked at General Motors for 32 years so he could put braces on the teeth of his five children; or my mother's sleepless nights worrying about us and her endless days shuffling us around, all the while putting three good meals on the table day after day after day...

My parents were both stellar examples of the inarguable goodness that can spring from modest backgrounds. My mother was one of ten children, growing up in a Germantown, Illinois family, whose father was killed in a livery accident with a team of horses. So in 1931, at the age of 41, my grandmother became a single mother of ten children, in the already difficult days when America was still reeling from the effects of the Great Depression. As was the case almost one hundred percent of the time back then, Grandpa made the money while Grandma raised the kids.

But this all changed in the two-week period between the accident and his death from a ruptured spleen.

So with the help of her adult sons, my grandmother started a milk hauling business. And with the help of her daughters, she tended her home at the same time. Years later, when my mother shared the story, she explained that they were certainly not the wealthiest in town, but because of team work and faith in God, they survived.

My grandmother was a determined and successful business woman who taught her children the value of hard work and saving their money. If personal resilience and the ability to overcome obstacles is a trait within our DNA, I hope my grandma Beckmann passed on half of hers to the generations that followed.

I've seen those same traits in my mother, the sweetest, kindest, warmest mom anyone could have...and one who has known her own share of obstacles. Four months into her marriage to my father, she found him almost lifeless, overcome with carbon-monoxide poisoning and passed out on the seat of their car—an accident while attaching the city sticker on a cold January morning in 1948. She nursed him back to health...and possibly listened to a litany of complaints for the entire year that he was remanded to a strict vegetarian diet. But she felt that if he couldn't eat meat, then she wouldn't either and spent those same 365 days with nothing but veggies. I'm sure she saw it as a simple and logical solution, very little sacrifice involved. I like to see it as that wonderful Beckmann DNA promising the trickle-down effect. Like *her* mother, my mom has always been sensible and adaptable, wise with money. Her message was simple: spend less than you make. Such a basic premise, but it is one of the most fundamental keys to financial survival and ultimate success.

My father came from a family of four children in Damiansville, Illinois. His mother died shortly after the birth of his younger sister, and he and his three siblings were raised with the care of an aunt who moved in to help Grandpa while he worked the farm. For *good times* they turned to baseball and music...*lots* of music. They lived a simple life but worked hard, eating what was grown, milking cows, and butchering cattle. But mixed in with that my dad developed and nurtured a lifetime love of music — playing guitar, trumpet, and keyboards until about 2 years before his death.

Image

The carbon monoxide accident as a young man nearly killed him, but with mom's constant nursing he survived — not left untouched by it though and not without struggles. The incident virtually destroyed his short-term memory, and the simplest tasks were sometimes very challenging for him. If mom sent him on an errand, one of us kids would usually go along so we could remind him what needed to be done. And I didn't know until after his death, but Mom told me how "the accident" changed his personality. Not for the worse, per se, just different. Before his accident he was energetic and ambitious. After, he became more laid back and at times even lethargic.

Still, he persevered. While working for General Motors in St. Louis he operated a forklift, feeding the assembly line and unloading rail cars. *And,* he was a musician. He started a band in the 1960s which lasted for well over 30 years, a very successful dance band with a tremendous following. I was always very proud to see him perform on stage and had the privilege of sharing that stage as his drummer for many years. As a teenager, I didn't always think it was the coolest thing to do, but looking back I wouldn't trade it for anything.

I learned a lot about money while playing in his band. I was paid well—about $60 per night—and that was really good money for a 16-year old in 1979. New Year's Eve jobs were especially good, when he would pay his musicians $100 for the holiday gig. One particular New Year's Eve day I was playing basketball with my buddies on an outdoor court. For safety's sake I decided to move Dad's car a little farther away from missed rebounds and wild passes. I hastily jumped in the car, not bothering to close the door; and while backing up, the door jammed itself in the ditch and proceeded to be ripped from its hinges. There was nothing I could say except, "Sorry Dad, I ripped the door off your car." But he didn't get upset with me—the solution was simple enough when he said, "Tonight you're working for nothing." Actually, I was paid my $100 for that New Year's Eve booking and for a while thought maybe he'd relented. However, the next week we went to the salvage yard and, sure enough, we found a door for that car that I had to buy with my easy-come-easy-go $100. Lesson learned.

I had a very basic but also very stable childhood, and my parents practiced what they preached: work hard, save your money, say your prayers, and be nice to others. The rest will fall into place.

Image

That's about as much as you'll learn about me and my extended family background. This book was never meant to be an autobiography. But to be a good funeral director, I've always felt that you need the simple traits I was fortunate enough to learn as a young man. Perhaps the funeral director in your town is much the same.

I hope so.

Notes

_____

_____

_____

_____

_____

_____

_____

_____

_____

_____

_____

Chapter 3

"Vulnerability"

Our media seem to think that every person who walks through the door of a funeral home is *vulnerable* because there has been a death in the family — that every death is tragic and consumers can't think clearly when they are "devastated." As you may have learned through personal experience, not every death is tragic. In fact, most families whom I have guided through the years are thinking very clearly. In many cases, they are arranging the funeral of a relative who died in a nursing home, very old and afflicted with dementia…or perhaps a victim of a cancer that has ravaged their body.

These are the family members who have been grieving for weeks, months or years; and while dealing with the unavoidable feelings of loss and sadness they also hold an element of relief that the battle—the suffering—is over. They are not vulnerable. They are uninformed consumers, perhaps, but they are not vulnerable. They just don't know the difference between a bronze casket and one made of 20 gauge steel.

I made funeral arrangements with a woman whose husband just passed away after a long illness. She and her daughters walked into my selection room and carefully studied each and every casket. They asked intelligent questions and I dutifully answered each one honestly. After about 45 minutes (another great virtue of a funeral director is patience), the wife of the deceased was struggling between two hardwoods: a solid cherry (expensive) and a poplar (much less costly, yet very attractive.) I told her I would be very comfortable putting my own father in the poplar. Sold. It's a good thing I'm my own boss. I could've been fired working for someone else. Would I have made a bigger profit with the cherry? Absolutely—but I slept very well that night.

A fellow funeral director told me about an experience he'll never forget. A woman walked in to make funeral arrangements for her husband. Although he was sincere in offering his condolences by saying "You have my sympathy," her response was, "The last thing I need is your sympathy." This woman was not vulnerable. She was angry. And the angrier one is, the more defensive one will be..."You're not going to screw me..."

Another gentleman lost his wife suddenly. She was in her early 50s with twin teenage daughters. As the father of teenage daughters, I know firsthand how much it helps to have their mom around. There are times when my wife solves problems quickly and efficiently, while I just imagine what I would've done in her absence. I know I'm a good father, but nothing takes the place of Mom when the girls "have issues." This father was now faced with those problems and I'm sure many more yet unforeseen.

His parents, the girls' grandparents, walked in before him. He was still in the car, putting off the inevitable. His mother introduced herself and said, "Mike's angry. It'll take him a little while to come in." Angry does not equal vulnerable. As a matter of fact, it's just the opposite. Again, "You're not going to screw me..." When he finally did walk into my office, I made an extra effort to make him feel at ease. As funeral directors, we can't do or say anything to take away the hurt—no one can—but we can make a bad situation just a little more tolerable if we are polite, good listeners, compassionate, yet direct without being condescending. By the end of the arrangement conference and a final bill about $4000 less than anticipated, Mike was at ease.

Batesville Casket Company makes a casket called the A 40 Primrose (about $3000). It's an 18 gauge steel casket with crepe interior. They also make the same casket in Solid Bronze for $7000. My casket sales rep obviously wanted me to carry the Bronze; but with a wife, two kids, and two mortgages, I opted for the 18 gauge.

One day a prominently wealthy local citizen came in to make funeral arrangements for his mother. "The Primrose" was located at the far corner of the room, and from a distance he simply pointed and said, "I want that one...That's Mom." For a moment I thought "I could've sold the Bronze...he can afford it." This man was a fine example of not knowing the difference in caskets, and an equally fine example of not needing to care about the cost. But most people do care. And they should: because most families can't afford such a purchase without even basic regard for price.

The point I'm trying to make, is that this person certainly wasn't vulnerable. He wasn't even put in the position to *be* vulnerable. He was experiencing the darker version of relief, accepting the death of his ailing mother, seeing it as the end of her suffering and an end to part of his own. He had the funds to do as he wished. Who am I to stop him?

Although I mentioned the many families who are not completely devastated with the death, there are still too many instances when the opposite is true. I am talking about the death of a small child, a teenager, or a parent with young children. In my years as a funeral director, perhaps one of the most difficult situations was handling arrangements with families who have lost a child to SIDS, or Sudden Infant Death Syndrome. I cannot imagine putting a baby to bed one evening and walking in the next morning only to find the child lifeless. I simply can't.

I have made arrangements with the parents of two sons, one of whom killed the other in an argument, knowing that the family was burying one son that day but mourning the death of two. One of my best friends lost one of his three boys while the boy and his buddies were swimming in a backyard pool. It was an unexplainable drowning at a well-chaperoned pool party for a team of Little Leaguers. Why? We don't know, but those of us with faith – just like this boy's parents -- know someday we will have the answer.

Some of my other more memorable experiences in the arrangement office include working with the parents of a 12-year old girl, brutally murdered by some scumbag who doesn't deserve to breathe the air you and I enjoy. I have also guided a legally blind woman with three young children, whose husband, recently graduated from medical school, was killed in a traffic accident.

When one of the children was crying uncontrollably, her uncle said, "What do you need? I'll get you anything you want." Her only reply was a sobbing, "I want my Daddy back." Those are the funerals I pray to never have—then pray to never have repeated—but it invariably happens anyway.

People ask me all the time, "How do you do what you do?" The answer was learned from experience, not in mortuary school. When I'm working with families such as those described above, I just try to remember how much more difficult it is for them being the family who lost a child or a young parent...how much they need the objectivity of someone who can stand further away from the pain to help them through the process. Does that keep it from breaking my heart? No. But I'm the one who can go home that night and hug his wife and kids. How selfish would it be for me to dread my job while the families I serve are grieving over the loss of a spouse or a child?

Realizing that many families *are* vulnerable, most of us in the funeral profession would never take advantage of it. Unfortunately, today we have so many funeral homes which are part of large corporations, those with quotas to meet and reports to file with upper management. Large conglomerates have come into small towns and bought out the "little guys," employing micro managers who don't seem to know when to back off. Too often these days you don't see the owner of the local funeral home in church, at the grocery store or at the summertime festivals because he is sitting behind a big desk in another state.

When you have to make funeral arrangements one of those statistical three times in your life, know a little about the funeral home you have selected. Are they locally owned? If not, that's okay, but find out by whom they are owned. Who is your funeral director? How long has he been doing this? Does he show genuine compassion, is he patient, does he allow you to make well thought out decisions?

If you are not comfortable with him, please ask to work with someone else. And if there *is* no one else, go to another funeral home. Just because he did the embalming doesn't lock you in, and the new funeral home will make arrangements for the transfer. His ego will only hurt a little, and your comfort level is much more important.

One other thing to remember: certain things are not about the deceased or your friends. They're about you. If you want the funeral on Friday because you don't want to wait, then do it Friday. Even though more of your friends and associates could attend a Saturday funeral and may try to influence your decision, it's your friends who need to re-arrange *their* schedules, not you. You have more than enough to be dealing with. And from a financial standpoint, the cemetery and the vault delivery fee are more expensive for Saturday funerals.

Don't be vulnerable. Be informed. Make sure you know all of the figures. There is so much more to be considered, and I intend to teach you everything I can.

Let's get started.

Notes

_____

_____

_____

_____

_____

_____

_____

_____

_____

_____

Chapter 4

Federal Intervention

The Federal Trade Commission is very strict with our industry — to the point where it's actually tacky to follow all of their rules. Although we are required to hand out our "General Price List" when the family walks through the front door, I don't know of any of us who do.

How impersonal.

When we respond to a death at a residence, if the subject of cost is brought up by the family, we are required to hand them a price list at that moment. I'll admit this is where I sometimes bend the rules. If they ask, I can give them approximate costs by adding in my head. And by doing so, I don't look like money is all I care about. "Did you see that guy? He carries a price list for funerals in his coat pocket!"

I make it a point to show all of my families the price list, but at a time I feel is most appropriate...before they select a casket, vault, urn or other merchandise. This way they have a figure that's fresh in their heads about what they might spend. Before walking into the "Selection Room," know what you have spent so far. By now you have selected all of your funeral arrangements, and those selections cost money. This is known as the "Service Charge."

Before 1984, funeral homes in this country didn't itemize their charges. They had one price for services with a casket. The FTC felt this was unfair to the consumer, making it too difficult to compare prices. Much to the chagrin of the funeral industry, the FTC enacted what is known as "The Funeral Rule."

Funeral directors had the typical reaction...too much government. *We've been doing this for years. We don't want to change. It'll be too much work, etc.* Of any profession I know, the funeral profession is slowest to change. The industry itself however, is forcing the change upon us. Cremation is on the rise. There is much less tradition. Funeral home loyalty went out the window as society's reluctance to spend came into play. Funeral consumers are actually "shopping around" as any informed consumer should. Hence, the feds intervened and said we need to simplify our pricing.

Funeral directors ended up with a surprise. By itemizing they learned three things: 1) it didn't make the services any less costly, 2) they actually learned what it costs to provide those services....and it wasn't cheap, and 3) the consumer will shop for the best deal, even at the time of a death.

Many years ago, a gentleman died and I got the call. It was in the middle of the night in a blinding snow storm, several miles out in the country. Prior to the days of Global Positioning Satellites and cell phones, our only option was to write down the directions given in the initial phone call and do the best we could. When I finally arrived, the widow said her husband wanted to be cremated and have no services. I told her that would be no problem, that she would simply need to come in the following day so we could complete the obituary, acquire death certificate information, sign the authorization to cremate, etc. She said she'd be there in the morning and she was.

After cremation, the cremated remains (ashes) are placed in what's known as a "temporary container." It's called temporary for marketing purposes only, implying that the consumer must purchase a "permanent" container, such as an expensive urn. I'll explain more of that later. At any rate, this widow chose not to purchase an urn at that time, and I completely understood. I remind people that cremation affords you the luxury of time. If you don't immediately know what to do with the ashes, you can decide later.

Several weeks passed when she called me and said, "Joe, I'd like to buy an urn. What does the Aristocrat Gold, # 100201 cost?" Do you think she was shopping around? At the time my cost was about $350, and I gave her a price of $700. That's right, 100% mark-up. The $350 was my profit in that call and I'm not ashamed of it. She told me my competitor down the street was going to sell it to her for $340, "But I'd like to get it from you." I understood her desire to be frugal, but there was suddenly no regard for the person with whom she had established trust, who trekked out into the snow storm in the middle of the night, who guided her with absolutely no pressure and treated her with kindness and compassion. For the briefest moment I wanted to ask her if she buys a steak at her local market then takes it to a restaurant to have it prepared. But instead I sent her to my competitor. If he wanted to lose money on it so I didn't get the sale, so be it.

Another virtue of a good funeral director is principle. Would I have been more compassionate if I had sold the urn at cost? Perhaps, but I have a business to run. There is a fine line between compassion and "taking it on the chin." It takes a lot of years to know the difference.

So for the last 26 years, funeral homes have changed with the consumers by itemizing such things as basic services of funeral director and staff, transfer of remains to funeral home, automobiles, embalming, use of facilities, and staff and equipment. The sum of these figures totals the "service charge." Basically, the service charge is the funeral home's operating expenses, or overhead...the word all business owners know. This is what it costs to run a business. And in the funeral business, this annual figure is divided into the average number of calls the funeral home will do in a year.

Every business has fixed expenses; those recurring bills which are always there regardless if you have revenue generating business. Principal, interest, salaries, insurance, auto loans, phone bills, utilities, and maintenance are but a few of these expenses which need to be paid on a monthly basis. If the sum of these bills is, for example, $50,000 per month ($600,000 annually), and the funeral home does an approximate volume of 150 calls per year, the service charge should be about $4000 per call.

So for every adult, casketed funeral the funeral home performs, the family will be charged approximately $4000 to cover the overhead involved in providing that funeral...the operating expense that ensures the hearse, lead car, and limo are clean, fueled, insured, and driven; the building is maintained with the yard mowed and the parking lot lighted and litter-free; staff is at the ready 24 hours a day; the embalmer is paid in addition to the owner (and sometimes previous owner).

As long as there is a demand for full-service funerals they will not get any less expensive. Before the rise in the cremation rate and other less traditional forms of disposition, this was all the funeral industry knew. Yes, funerals are expensive — because like any other business we cannot *stay* in business by losing money or simply breaking even. But at the end of the year, our profit margin is no greater than the restaurant, service station, clothing store or barber shop down the street. Hopefully, we'll show an 8% profit just like any other business. And that would be a very good year.

So the Funeral Rule was meant to aid the consumer — and it has. It clarifies exactly what it is that you are purchasing. However, it has also been of benefit to the funeral industry because it clarifies exactly what it is we are providing; notably itemized services and merchandise. And when added together, it's usually an expensive proposition. Yet if you are well-informed, you can make wise decisions which will save you money...and I intend for you to be *very* well-informed.

Notes

_____

_____

_____

_____

_____

_____

_____

_____

_____

_____

_____

Chapter 5

"Let's Go Shopping"

"Deathcare" is a term heard more frequently today, for the consumer no longer shops for funerals alone. The classic term "funerals" grows increasingly generic since the consumer is shopping for much more: body donations to science, direct cremations, immediate burials, private services, and other forms of disposition not having anything to do with an actual funeral or memorial service, which is an event with or without the body, when a life is celebrated.

So when you, the consumer, are planning for the inevitable, there are some things you need to know. When you call the funeral home on the telephone, the FTC requires the funeral home to quote prices if you ask. If they do not want to quote prices over the phone they are violating the law, and you should either report them, call another firm or both.

If you go to the funeral home for a personal visit, they are required to show and explain to you their general price list, which you may keep if you so desire. If you are shopping for a casket, they must show you a "casket price list." However, they are not required to allow you to keep it. Many times the casket pricelist will be laminated, indicating it is the property of the funeral home, which it is.

But I'd like to let you in on a little secret. Remember that $4000 figure I explained in the last chapter? Well, since more of you actually are shopping around, that figure is sometimes deflated in the interest of competition. But does the funeral home lose money in providing those services for less? Not if it can be made up with the merchandise sale. So if you want to know the clear-cut bottom line, make sure you know what the casket costs and if it is the exact model quoted from the other funeral home. If you are truly shopping, we usually have that figured out even if you don't admit it. So just ask us, and we'll tell you it's the R 59 Coretta, for example. This way you can go to the next firm and get an accurate quote on the bottom line.

Of course the casket companies don't support failure to recover true overhead; nor do I. I feel a funeral home should recoup its operating expenses and keep the cost of the merchandise lower. Why? Because the internet has affected nearly every industry around the world, and the funeral industry is not immune. You can purchase a casket online and have it shipped to the funeral home, but something you should remember: that online merchant can't pick up the body, transport, embalm, prepare obituaries or sign the death certificate. That's the job of your funeral director.

With that being said, funeral homes have become more competitive in an effort to counteract the online leverage—and we have the blessing of the FTC. I'm talking about Package Pricing. It's the method of lumping all of the service charges into one "package," and providing this package when the merchandise is actually purchased from the funeral home. This package will be considerably less than if itemized. It is not a "discount" and cannot be presented as such, but must be specifically described on the General Price List. If all of the service charges are added individually, instead of the $4000 figure described earlier, it will add up to, for example, $4900.

What is the minimum profit a funeral home hopes to make with a casket sale? You guessed it: $900. So the family buys the casket from Costco and pays an additional $900 for services. It's completely legal and allows the funeral home to recover "the profit" they may have lost.

The American Legion Magazine ran an ad for a company that sold military-themed caskets out of a catalog. There was a gentleman from Edwardsville, Illinois, where my funeral home had been for the past 40 years, who wanted that casket for his impending death. He didn't look at it as side-stepping the funeral director; he simply saw it as a benefit for a veteran. It was a stainless steel casket which *retailed* for about $1200, while the *wholesale* cost on a stainless steel casket I carried was $1400. It is what it is. This casket was shipped to me at the time of death and I was informed by the family they had also purchased the vault from the same company. Ouch. It was a big funeral; I worked my tail off, and made zero profit. You see, it was before the days of Packaged Pricing.

In a case like this, beware of certain consequences. The vault will usually have the decedent's name on the top, and for the purposes of this story I'll say his name was

44

"Jones."As we all gathered at the cemetery, Mr. Jones' son noticed it had been spelled "Junes". He and I both kept it quiet, but I'll admit that it was tempting to point out that if I had been involved in that part of the service, I would've spelled the name correctly. At the conclusion of the services the son said to me, "Joe, I can't help but think you got screwed." I told him not to worry about it…

He was just carrying out his father's wishes.

Notes

Chapter 6

Goods & Services

The funeral contract is also known as "the Statement of Goods and Services." It is an actual contract which must be signed by the funeral provider and the person responsible for payment. It could be a legal size document with two carbon copies or it could be a contract generated by a computer. Regardless of how it is presented, every contract has the same three categories: Services, Merchandise and Cash Advances.

Let's start with Services. As you know by now, the itemized services are intended to cover the funeral home's operating expenses. But I need to explain each of these items separately.

Basic Services of Funeral Director & Staff"

- Consultation and arrangements with family, clergy, cemetery, florists, and others as required

- Preparation of, filing, and securing necessary notices, authorizations and permits

- Assistance with forms and 24-hour availability of staff.

"This fee will be added to the total cost of the funeral arrangements you select and is already included in our charge for direct cremation, immediate burials, and forwarding or receiving of remains."

This figure can range from $1200 to $2200. No matter what type of disposition is chosen, the funeral home will provide the above-mentioned service. Behind the desk and on paper there's just as much work with a direct cremation as there is with a full traditional funeral.

Because of this, the list of services noted above is labeled as a **"non-declinable option."** It's important to remember that every other item associated with the funeral contract is a **declinable option.** It's also important to remember that this fee will be listed as included with the charges of direct cremation and "Forwarding and Receiving Remains," which will be explained a little later.

"Embalming"

Except in certain cases, embalming is not required by law. Embalming may be necessary, however, if you select certain funeral arrangements such as a funeral with viewing. If you do not want embalming, you usually have the right to choose an arrangement that does not require you to pay for it, such as direct cremation or immediate burial.

The above is taken directly from my GPL (General Price List). The wording we use is very specific and highly scrutinized by the FTC. The FTC has been known to make surprise visits to see if we are in compliance; and while most funeral homes complain, I feel it keeps us honest, informed, and only enhances our credibility with the public.

I wish I had a dollar for every time I've been asked the question, "Is embalming a state law?" The answer is no. However, there are certain circumstances which would require embalming. Will there be a public viewing? If so, of course embalming is necessary and would have to be selected. An un-embalmed body is hazardous to anyone near it. In a matter of hours, the body starts to decompose and becomes offensive very quickly.

Neanderthal Man was the original undertaker. After his friend would lie still for a day or two, he started to smell. Then he started to turn green, and later black – after which he started to smell even worse. Finally, Neanderthal Man decided to dig a hole so he could cover up the smell (interment). After he discovered that by rubbing two sticks together he could build a fire, he put the body on it for the same reason (cremation).

The Egyptians learned to preserve the body and eliminate the odors without interment or cremation, and in doing so became our first embalmers – eventually discovering "entombment." Today's embalmers accomplish the same results with preservation, but instead of a 40-day process we can do it in about an hour and a half. Our method is not quite as thorough, but it is efficient. Embalming does not stop decomposition, it just retards (slows) it. Today's embalming methods decelerate decomposition long enough for the body to be viewed in a safe and sterile environment, but not forever. Still, in reality, under the right conditions an embalmed body can be recognizable years after burial. I'll explain more of that when we talk about caskets and vaults.

Jessica Mitford, author of the 1960s best seller, *The American Way of Death*, called embalming "barbaric." I strongly disagree. Embalming is simply a post-mortem procedure which preserves, cleanses, and sanitizes the deceased human body while retarding decomposition to allow for public viewing. It is a very sterile procedure performed in an operating room-like setting by highly trained personnel who take their jobs as seriously as an artist would his subject.

Imagine a person collapsing in front of you. An ambulance is called. This person, who could be your father or grandfather, is rushed to the hospital. You frantically follow the ambulance on its way to the emergency room. They whisk him into another area and work on him for the next hour, but to no avail. The doctors walk into the waiting room and inform you he has passed, despite their efforts, which included oxygen, IVs, G-tubes, and more. You ask to see him "one more time." They bring you in and you see him swollen in the neck and face, with dark and malodorous fluids leaking from his mouth and nose. It doesn't even look like him. What happened? This morning he was Dad. He got up, shaved, put on his clothes, ate breakfast, and went about his day. Now he is a stranger, lying on a stained hospital bed, his clothing ripped, covered in his own body fluids.

This is where the embalmer comes in. The deceased is taken back to the funeral home, placed on the operating table, removed of his torn and stained clothing, bathed, and then embalmed. Measures were taken to reduce the swelling and prevent the fluids from purging. The next day he is cosmetised and dressed in the clothing most appropriate, whether it's a suit and tie or a flannel shirt and blue jeans. Now he looks like Dad. Without embalming, the last picture in your mind would be of him in the hospital. Not a pleasant memory...and not the one you want to remember him by.

Another horrific example would be to discover the body of a friend or family member who has put a .22 caliber bullet through his forehead. I use the .22 as an example because the embalmer can actually restore this body to a viewable condition. You see, the entrance wound is the size of the bullet. The exit wound at the back of the head would require the most work. And that's the part no one will see. When we can reconstruct or restore their looks to a presentable manner, it can be an invaluable gift to the family. The body is given back.

Jessica Mitford had a true hatred of the entire funeral industry. In his book, *Bodies in Motion and at Rest,* Thomas Lynch explores the possible reasons for her angst. I consider Lynch's work to be a tremendous read by a talented author, poet, and funeral director. I highly recommend it—and if you enjoy this book half as much, I'll be satisfied.

"Does a body have to be embalmed if it will be cremated?" As the owner of a crematory, I get that question a lot. The answer, of course, is no. But we have another "however." You might expect us to have a lot of paperwork. You're right. And actually, there's considerably more with that of a cremation. Why? Because once the cremation is performed, all of the evidence is gone. So the death certificate has to be signed by either a physician or medical examiner/coroner, certifying the cause of death. Then the "Coroner's Permit to Cremate" is issued, followed by the "Permit for Disposition," which is issued by either the city registrar or county health department.

Even with today's "electronic filing," this paperwork can sometimes take several days to complete. Throw in a weekend or holiday and you'll add maybe another two days. Most funeral homes don't have refrigeration; and in this case they could require embalming. But I will say this: given similar circumstances, small town funeral homes usually will not require embalming. They would place the body in a cremation container (usually made of cardboard) and wheel it into the air-conditioned embalming room or another "holding area." Sort of "bending the rules" as it were. Large, corporate-owned funeral homes, however, (there's that word again) would probably view this as an opportunity to require embalming, and would not hesitate to charge for it. That's their right, but another subtle difference between the big guy and the little guy.

I could go on and on about other requirements for embalming, but I think you have the idea. The bottom line, embalming is *not* a state law and in many cases, **may be declined.** But if it is selected, could cost anywhere from $400 - $800.

"Other Preparation of Body"

"Besides embalming, Joe, what else do you 'have to do' to the body?"

"Well, we're not going to lay the body out naked. Also, if I don't apply some cosmetics, grandpa will actually *look* dead. I forgot to mention I had a major problem with leakage from the extra 100 pounds of edema (fluids) which is now escaping his body, so it took my apprentice and me an extra two hours to dress him."

Here's another one: "Remember how his driver's license indicated he was an organ donor? Well, the only organs taken were the bones in his legs and arms, and the skin off of his back. And you thought his heart would be transplanted to save someone else's life. So that took another two hours."

Are you still with me? Obviously, I would be less graphic and much more tactful with my explanations, but I hope you get the point. That's why it's called "other preparation of body" and that's why it might be an extra

$200 or more. These are functions performed by licensed embalmers who paid to go to school, and by the way, also have cast iron stomachs.

"Use of Facilities"

A visitation and/or funeral will be held in either the funeral home, church, cemetery chapel or even in a banquet center. Obviously there is a charge for this as well. You might wonder why the funeral home charges for a service at the church. After all, the funeral home doesn't own the church, and the director isn't paying for the electricity to run the lights. True. But he is delivering the casketed body, setting up the flowers (sometimes dozens of pieces), and has staff on hand to tend to the register book, memorial contributions, parking, etc. This charge can be anywhere from $250 to $600 per day.

One way to cut back on the facilities charge is to do everything in one day. As recently as twenty years ago, visitations (wakes) were held for two nights, followed by the funeral the next day. Talk about dragging things out. Funerals are painful enough. Besides dealing with the loss of a loved one, you're missing work, missing school, and rescheduling or canceling vacations.

Funerals are about celebrating a life. Visitations are about giving friends an opportunity to share a hug, shake a hand, and remember the good times. All of this can be accomplished in three hours, unless of course the deceased is a well known figure, which might prohibit my suggestion. But the average wake and funeral can be completed in one day, and it could save you $600.

"Automotive Equipment"

Typically, a funeral home will provide three cars for a funeral service — the hearse (obviously), limousine, and lead car. The lead car is just that...it leads the procession and is properly marked. The lead car is also usually transporting the minister to the cemetery unless, of course, he's in the back of the hearse, in which case another minister would be aboard.

The charge for these automobiles could be $150-$250 each. One of the easiest things to decline is the limousine. In small towns especially, the cemetery is near the funeral home and paying for a limousine is senseless. If you're into that and want to be treated royally for a day, use it. But practically speaking, it isn't necessary.

A gentleman from Edwardsville named Earl died. Earl had been a gravedigger for over 50 years. While families often choose a limousine for a select group of people, such as pallbearers or grandchildren, Earl's grandchildren decided to, in lieu of the limo, all pile into Earl's backhoe for the trip to the cemetery. There were probably seven or eight kids in that machine and they couldn't have had more fun. Hey, "We Put The *Fun* In Funeral." And they saved $150.

This may surprise you, but the hearse is declinable. "Well, what would we put the casket in, Joe?" One answer might be the back of your pick-up truck, if you desire. Obviously this doesn't happen often, but it has. I was working a funeral one day when the family decided to put the young man's casket in the back of his pick-up truck. We pulled the hearse out of line, put it in the garage, and took it off the bill. And it couldn't have been more appropriate. You see, funeral directors are all about "personalizing" the funeral. Casket companies give us all sorts of ways to personalize, all at the added expense of the consumer. But, what could be more personal than using one's own vehicle for his last ride?

Another vehicle may be defined as a "service utility vehicle." This is the funeral home van which is probably transporting flowers to the grave. Usually it is marked as "included," but trust me, it's built in to the service charge.

"Receiving Remains from Another Funeral Home"

When a funeral home gets a call from a funeral home in another state to pick up a casketed body at the airport, transport to the "receiving funeral home" and make arrangements for its burial at a local cemetery, this is called "Receiving Remains." This charge could be anywhere from $1200 - $2000. You might think that's a lot of money for such a small amount of work; but again, it's not cheap to own a hearse, insure it, put it on the road, pay a driver, assume the liability, etc. It's just the cost of doing business.

There's also the task at hand of coordinating the arrangements with the original funeral home, the airlines, the local cemetery, florist, minister, vault company and any other details and entities it may entail. And let's not forget the main job. We have to actually go to the cemetery, set the casket, and direct the service. This alone could take two hours from start to finish. And in most states, you have to be a licensed funeral director to provide this service.

It seems so easy; a trip to the airport and a trip to the cemetery. But there is so much more involved. These are all things not obvious to the consumer, but very obvious to the funeral home owner.

"Forwarding Remains to Another Funeral Home"

If you have a winter home in Arizona, but primarily reside in the Midwest, for example, you should make arrangements ahead of time with your funeral home in the Midwest to "forward your remains" home. One of the biggest mistakes you can make when dealing with an out of town death, is to call *two* funeral homes instead of only one. Let the receiving funeral home, i.e. the one in the Midwest, be the one to make all of the arrangements. This could save you up to $1000 or more.

If your intention is to have the funeral at "Midwest Funeral Home" but you personally call "Arizona Funeral Home," Arizona Funeral Home will view this as "a call," and you will be subjected to some of their service charges.

Conversely, if you called Midwest Funeral Home and say, "Joe, my husband died. He's at Memorial Hospital in Anytown, AZ, and I need to get him home so we can have the funeral at St. Boniface Catholic Church in Edwardsville. What do I do now?" The answer is, "You just did it. All you needed to do is call me." At this point, I will call a funeral home or an embalming service near the place of death and they will be subcontracted to do the removal and embalming. They will also arrange for the flight and transport the body to the airport.

When we subcontract some of the work, it's done for a fraction of the price because only one funeral home is collecting the information for the obituaries and death certificates and performing other administrative duties associated with the death.

When you walk into "Arizona Funeral Home" and say, "My husband died. I need you to get him back to Illinois." The funeral director will ask you to be seated and some $2500 later (much more if he talks you into purchasing the casket from him, which is not professionally courteous) he'll be on his way. But if "Midwest Funeral Home" is called instead, it will be closer to $1200-$1500 including the airline charges, because they are performing all of these administrative duties.

Only call one funeral director; the one back home, the one you've known for years; the one whose kids went to school with your kids, the one you've seen grocery shopping and at church.

I hope I've made my point.

Chapter 7

Merchandise (Caskets)

The term "merchandise" includes a variety of items: caskets, vaults, register book packages, thank you cards, urns, flowers, and jewelry. That's right, jewelry. We can take a thumbprint of the deceased, keep it in a file, and at anytime in the future, you may come back and order a charm with mom's thumbprint on it, or a cigarette lighter with the same. Key fobs are another option, as are pendants with a portion of the ashes, which can be worn around the neck.

"What a cute necklace. What's in it?"

"Oh, thank you. It's Mom."

Some people think it's creepy. I say to each his own. If there's a demand, we'll provide. The list goes on and on....

I recently met with a family who wanted a direct cremation with no service. "It was Dad's wishes. He didn't want us to overspend." Then they proceeded to buy $2000 worth of jewelry. I have information on "thumbies" in my arrangement office. I don't even push it. It sells itself. Invariably, someone will pick up a brochure and say "I want this. How much does it cost?" I tell them the price and they usually order at least two. Is this crazy? Some would think...but it's not for me to judge. The industry is changing and we need to change with it.

I'd like to think that every funeral director "teaches" while making funeral arrangements, explaining all of your choices. But most people don't care what "cathodic protection" is, or if the bottom of the casket has a seamless weld. They care about how it looks. Is it pretty? Is it feminine? Is it masculine? Does the interior go with Mom's dress? Well, on most selection room floors, all of the really expensive caskets answer those questions with a resounding "yes."

Casket company representatives advise funeral directors how to arrange their floors — what caskets to put where, how to highlight certain "price points," what kind of lighting, etc. And they should. That's their job. Most older funeral directors would rather have those reps stay out of their rooms, but in these days of marketing, merchandising, and price shopping, the younger funeral directors see the value in their advice. Funeral home owners would like to show a profit at the end of the year, and that profit comes directly from the merchandise they sell. And that's okay. It has to come from somewhere. If funeral homes didn't show a profit, we would have no funeral homes, and then what would we do with the dead? It's called "undertaking" for a reason. It truly is at times a very unpleasant task and it's a job not meant for many.

I will share something with you most funeral home owners would not: the mark-up on caskets. I do this not to upset funeral home owners because it shouldn't. If you're ashamed of your profit go work for the Peace Corp. I have two daughters to send to college, two weddings to pay for, and a retirement to think about someday, hopefully before I'm 65.

We have a right to make a profit so here it is. If the wholesale cost of a casket is $1000, most funeral homes will retail it for about $2500. That's a 2.5 mark-up. The rule of thumb is: the higher the wholesale, the lower the mark-up. So if another casket wholesales for $2000, the mark-up might be around 2.0, so that casket would retail for $4000. A $3000 casket might have a 1.8 mark-up, so that casket would be $5400. You get the idea.

You might think this is unfair. You might think they're making too much profit. But think of it this way: most funeral homes do a volume of less than 100 "death calls" per year. So, for the sake of example, let's say 75 calls. Of those 75 calls, 24 will be cremation and another three will be anatomical donations — which means this funeral home actually sold only 48 caskets.

Most people don't buy coppers and bronzes anymore, so the average margin might be around $1200. That's an annual profit of $57,600, or a little over 9% based on revenue of $600,000. This would be considered a really good year. It's not a fortune in earnings, and is just as deserved as that of our fellow business owners on Main Street. If you keep in mind that to acquire this profit your small town funeral director is on-call 24 hours a day, seven days a week, if we can't make 9% on our money, we should probably be doing something else.

Casket room floors are merchandised no differently than a lot of retail stores, with lighting and placement of product being very important. That's why upon entering the selection room, the caskets which make the most profit are highlighted. But you have to remember, just because you don't see a particular casket doesn't mean it's not available. Most funeral homes can receive next-day delivery, and if they are too far from the distribution site, it may be in storage. You need to ask.

Also, if you really like the solid bronze casket with the velvet interior but don't want to spend $7000, ask if they have a similar looking 18 gauge. It will be less than half the cost and no one will know the difference.

This brings me to another point. You, the consumer, need to know the difference in caskets, why they cost what they do, and what you can do to make sensible decisions when selecting one. There are basically two types of caskets: metal and wood. From most expensive to least, the metal caskets are made from the following materials: bronze, copper, stainless steel, 16 gauge, 18 gauge, and 20 gauge steel. The key to this rating is the higher the gauge of steel, the thinner the metal. That's why 20 gauge caskets cost less than 16 gauge. Steel caskets rust over time, precious metal caskets do not. Does it matter? You be the judge. I personally think it doesn't, and I'll give you some reasons very soon.

From most expensive to least, wooden caskets are made from the following species: mahogany, walnut or cherry, oak, maple, pecan, pine, and poplar. The wooden caskets you see on the selection room floor will be polished, well lit, made of the finest woods and have a plush, velvet interior. The corners of the casket will be inter-changeable so it can be personalized. You have many themes: golfer, fisherman, gardener, mother, father, religious, military....you name it, we can personalize it.

Heck, we'll do four different corners if Mom or Dad had several interests. My most memorable experience came about five years ago, when a family asked for four different corners: fisherman, hunter, Dad, and a Christian cross. What made this memorable is where these corners were to be placed. They requested the fisherman and hunter be on the front where everyone could see. Dad and the Christian cross were on the back, because apparently they were not as important to him. I thought about how I wanted my own priorities reflected. I then told my wife, Cheryl, if she ever has to select corners for my casket, put Dad and the Christian cross on the front.

Most funeral homes will display 15 - 20 caskets on their floor; but once again, you will not see everything that is available. You will see the casket they would like you to buy, but you might not see a price range with which you feel comfortable. There are very attractive 20 gauge steel caskets and there are very attractive poplar caskets. You just don't commonly see them, because they do not have the highest margins. Most funeral homes will remove a "cheaper" casket from its floor if it sells too much. I'll hear the funeral director say, "This one's too pretty" or "This one needs to be in a painted finish so it looks cheaper."

But you have choices. Tell the funeral director the price range in which you are comfortable, and if you don't see the casket in the room ask to see a catalog. He can probably show you books from three different companies and you'll soon have many more choices of those in your price range. And remember, your funeral director should always remain patient. If he isn't, ask to work with someone else. You should never feel pressured.

For me, the worst part of making funeral arrangements is taking the family into this room. I've never sold cars, but I would assume it could be fun. Selling boats is probably fun. Selling caskets is *not* fun. First of all, I'm a terrible salesman. I have a tremendous respect for those who make a living on commission. I would fail miserably since I can never "close the deal." No pressure from me. I truly feel I am an excellent funeral director *because* I'm a terrible salesman. I sell down more than I should—but as I said earlier in this book, I sleep well at night.

I just don't feel there's a need to spend $7000 on a casket when you can purchase one for thousands less, which looks just as nice, and will be buried in three days never to be seen again. I can't tell you how many times throughout the years I have heard a family say when selecting a casket for Dad, years after Mom died, "the only thing I remember is it was kind of a bronze color." They don't say, "Yes, Joe, do you still carry the Aegean Copper?...Because we loved that one." And if the family doesn't remember, who the heck else will? Funerals are not the time to impress anyone, anyway.

One thing I hear a lot from families selecting a casket is the question, "Does it seal?" It seems that "the sealer" casket is of more quality than the "non-sealer," hence the need to spend more. I also hear: "Well it's going to be in a vault, so we don't need a sealer casket." The truth is, you don't "need" anything. It comes down to what your beliefs are religiously, if you have any, and how you personally feel about how much the body is protected after burial.

You can spend $10,000 on a solid bronze casket, put it in a $9000 concrete vault with a bronze liner and the body will still decompose. You see, there is this thing called anaerobic bacteria; the bacteria which grow without the presence of oxygen. They'll have a party in such an environment. Also, the body is 75-85% water, and that water will escape to the bottom of the casket in a matter of months.

Or you could spend $1500 on a 20 gauge non-sealer with a polished finish, put it in an $800 concrete box which the cemetery requires and let the aerobic bacteria take over. (That's the bacteria which grow in the presence of oxygen). What about the $10,000 mahogany? Wooden caskets do not seal. You'll get more protection in a sandwich bag.

You see, if you're interested in protecting the body after death, you'll never get away from decomposition.

That's not what God intended when He made us. Sealer or non-sealer, metal or wood, bronze or copper, we *will* return to the earth. It just might take a little longer in some cases.

Chapter 8

Merchandise (Vaults)

Anyone who has ever made funeral arrangements has encountered the one member of the family who seems to be the authority on all subjects. I will be asked, "What about Social Security? Won't I get a death benefit?" Before I can answer, this person will quickly say, "Yeah. Everybody gets $250." It's at this time I dig deep to find my tact and politely correct him or her by saying, "Well, Social Security pays $255, but only to a surviving spouse or dependent child, provided the decedent is qualified." That statement usually assures the family that I know what I'm talking about.

But this same person seems to be an authority on burial vaults, too. "We have to buy a vault, Mom, it's a state law." Since I have already dug deep and found my tact, I'll leave it in a place easily accessible. I reach for it again and politely say, "No, it's not a state law, but the cemetery you've

73

chosen requires the casket be placed in at least a minimum container." But what I really want to say is, "Sit down and shut up, Jethro, I do this for a living!"

Thank goodness I keep track of my tact.

Buying a vault is less complicated than buying a casket, thankfully, but there still is much to know. Instead of 20 different choices, you'll *only* have about nine—when, in reality, it ought to be only three...good, better, best. Your nine choices will range in price from about $800 for that concrete box to approximately $9000 for the bronze vault with the double liner. In my career, I have never sold the latter and am convinced I never will. That's because I don't even offer it. I just don't believe in it.

In my funeral home/crematory, I've taken a much different approach to everything about this business. I will explain that more thoroughly later in the book. Unlike other funeral homes, I show only three types of containers: a concrete box; a concrete vault with a liner that provides "basic" protection; and a concrete vault which is heavier, made with a slightly better liner, and is a little more aesthetically pleasing. The vault will be seen for 15 minutes at the committal service, so that third feature is important to those who want a better visual or place significant value on impressing their friends.

You'll notice I didn't call the first unit a "vault" because it isn't. It's a box; a box big enough to hold a casket. It also has a lid which fits on top but does not seal anything. Although buying this box or a more sophisticated vault is not a state law, the cemetery will usually require it for grave maintenance purposes. Simply put, graves sink, which makes it hard to cut grass. The grave doesn't sink as badly if the casket is encased. If you're interested in saving money and your beliefs permit it, ask the funeral director if an outer container is needed. Truthfully speaking, most families I've worked with do select one even if not required. This box will not keep out all of the water, but it will keep out the dirt and protect the casket from the weight of the earth.

Wilbert Vault Company makes a vault called The Monticello. It's a fine vault made by a fine company which has been around for a long time. This vault will sometimes be described by the funeral director as a minimum vault providing "basic" protection. The word "basic" is used to imply that, although this vault is good, there are better vaults. But don't be fooled by the terminology. This vault is made of concrete, has a seamless liner, and has a lid with a tongue & groove seal. It's more than basic. It'll provide enough protection that Wilbert will give you a 75-year warranty, which is laughable to some. Who really cares? Will we dig it up when we're 108 years old?

The Monticello is usually displayed in a very bland gray color. The vaults which are more expensive will look much nicer on display. But the Monticello can be painted to match the casket. They will even highlight with gold or silver sparkles. The person's name will be on top and will have an appropriate emblem to go with it. This vault will usually retail for $1000 to $1400, depending on where you live.

If you want the casket to be somewhat protected and don't like the idea of ground water penetrating the seams of the concrete, this vault is an excellent choice. Don't let anyone tell you it isn't. Long before I became a funeral director, my uncle delivered and installed Wilbert burial vaults. He swore by that vault—and earlier this year when he died, my cousins chose The Monticello. I know that's what he would've wanted.

Merchandise (Vaults)

The next vault I will describe is called "The Venetian." It is two steps up from The Monticello. I skipped the one in between, "The Continental," because there's very little difference between it and The Monticello—it's slightly heavier, a little nicer to look at, and a couple hundred bucks more because it's made with more concrete. If you're into looks and want to impress your friends for 15 minutes at the cemetery, which I don't agree with, The Venetian is the one for you. Of course it's made of concrete, has a "marbelon" liner, and has a carapace. It's a beautiful vault, but in my opinion does not offer much more protection. This vault will cost in the range of $1400 - $1900, again depending on the area.

There are four or five more vaults above these, all heavier, fancier, double lined, and *much* more expensive. Do I show them? No. And it would cost me nothing to do so. I would be provided the samples and they wouldn't take up much space. I just can't. If the family I'm serving truly wants additional options, I have a pricelist for these vaults, but I will be the first to ensure them of the value in one of the first three. How can I justify a copper-lined vault when it is more than even I chose for my own father?

Vault companies charge a fee to install the vault. Oftentimes they set the tent and chairs for the committal service as well. This fee can be a minimum of $250 and much more if it's a Saturday or holiday. When you see the price of the vault, this fee is not included because it's a service as opposed to tangible merchandise. Depending on the state in which you live, you're only taxed on the merchandise. Therefore, this fee is treated as a cash advance, which will be discussed in a subsequent chapter. When selecting the vault or concrete box, be sure to ask about this fee. You'll want to know how much more will be added to the bill.

Good, better, best. Arranging funerals can be complicated enough, especially when emotions tend to get in the way. Why complicate it even more by offering nine different vaults. Good, better, best. Concrete box, lined vault or lined vault that's a little fancier.   All three serve different purposes and do the job that needs to be done.

There are other types of vaults, such as steel vaults which *envelop* the casket. The casket sets on a base and the lid and sides come down from the top. I am not as familiar with these but I can say this; if you have to select one of them select one of the three least expensive. Have the funeral director explain exactly how it will function. Tell him if you have any concerns, what they are, and then choose the one that best meets with your approval. You don't need to spend $2000 extra for added protection. You'll get all you need with one of the bottom three.

Notes

Chapter 9

Clothing & Flowers

"We'd like the flowers to match Mom's dress." This is a statement I've heard countless times so I thought I'd talk about both in the same chapter. If you've never seen the clothing, morbidly known as "burial garments," provided by a funeral home, it's exactly as you would imagine. Varying shades of pink, blue, and green with lace collars, high necklines, long sleeves and, you guessed it, slit down the back. Because it's virtually impossible to dress a deceased human body, stiff from the embalming procedure, without the assistance of a scissors. A man's suit is less morbid, because it's just a suit; an overpriced suit, but a suit nonetheless.

The dresses are also overpriced and, did I say they were morbid? When asked about clothing, I *always* suggest that the decedent's own clothing be provided if at all possible. You might wonder, do some actually *not* have any clothing? The answer is yes; most notably older folks who die in a nursing home. Many times they have nothing but hospital gowns and sweat pants. If the family needs a dress or a suit, or jeans and a tee shirt, I suggest they go to the local department store and look for something. If the funeral home sells them the clothing, they have to make $100 on it. And to be fair, you'd do much better going to Wal-Mart. Remember how I said the vault will only be seen for about 15 minutes and then forgotten? Well, the clothing will be seen for several hours, but again, who are you trying to impress?

Let's be practical.

"Do I need to bring in underwear, shoes and socks?" Yes. It's a human body and we funeral directors treat it with respect. I say "it" because everything that made that person Mom or Dad is gone, but it's still Mom or Dad. I should know. I embalmed my own father—and my father-in-law. And like the 2000 other bodies I've embalmed and dressed in my career, they had on underwear, shoes and socks.

A family came in many years ago, and upon my suggestion brought in the gentleman's suit, along with his shirt, tie, underwear, shoes, and socks. Or so I thought. They told me, "His socks are in his pocket." While dressing him, however, I couldn't find his socks anywhere. I looked in every pocket I saw but found no socks. Every funeral home has a cabinet full of extra undergarments. I'd like to think it's all new, but I'm sure that through the years extra clothing is brought in and a collection is formed. We'll let no poor soul be buried without clothing, even if it is someone else's. Well, I reached into my cabinet and put on a brand new pair of "goldtoes." He was dressed, cosmetics looked great, the funeral home was clean, sidewalks were swept, and I was ready for the viewing.

After seeing her husband for the first time in his casket, the widow turned to me and said, "Joe. Please come here."

As if summoned by my boss—because the family *is* my boss—I warily stepped forward and said, "Yes, Melba?"

"I told you his socks were in his pocket."

"I know," I said, "but I couldn't find them. I thought you were mistaken."

"No," she said, "they're still there." She then pointed to his *lapel* pocket and there, clear as day for everyone to see, were his socks, sticking straight up, looking like a lapel handkerchief (to *me*, anyway). I guess I didn't look closely enough. Thankfully, they got a good laugh out of it.

Bring in the deceased person's clothing...or go out and buy some — but don't overspend. Remember, it will only be seen for a short while.

Flowers are an interesting subject for the funeral director, and you would think his relationship with local florists would be one of peace and serenity. After all, he sends a lot of business to the florist. But the relationship is sometimes strained. Usually there are many more floral shops than funeral homes in the same town, and they all compete for funeral business. Just like weddings, people have come to see funeral flowers as an expected and desired expense.

I've seen many funeral directors grumble about selling a cheap casket, only to have the florist show up with

$1000 worth of flowers. I try to remember it's all about priorities. I'm just pleased to get the funeral because, like florists, we have competition ourselves.

Funeral directors will usually give you a choice: you can order the flowers (casket spray and other family pieces) or they can order the flowers for you and include them on the bill. *Put them on the bill,* choice B, is usually selected — which means we'll pay the florist for you. Isn't that nice? The florist gets their money and we could get stiffed (no pun intended). It's all about service; and if there was ever a service-oriented business, it's the funeral business. Do you see how the relationship can sometimes become strained?

Some funeral homes will actually have a "rental" casket spray. That's right, I said rental. It's a silk arrangement purchased by the funeral home that's used over and over again. They'll have one for each season, making the "rental" aspect less obvious since cattails wouldn't look right in December. But still, I personally have never owned a rented casket spray because it seems so impersonal. I like being practical, not cheap...and there's a big difference. Get some fresh flowers. You don't have to overspend, but a couple hundred dollars will add beauty to a sad situation. If

$200 is too much for your budget, you can get a nice arrangement, only smaller and in a vase, for $75. It's a nice touch and it's not that much. Besides, if you chose option B to *put them on the bill,* the funeral home took care of it. You can pay them within 30 days.

I can think of one more *big* reason for strained relationships, and it has to do with that one line in the obituary, "in lieu of flowers, donations can be made... "

Chapter 10

Urns

First of all, let's be sure you know just exactly what "ashes" are. Of course, I'm talking about the cremated remains of a deceased human being. The term "ashes" is somewhat misleading. When I think of ashes, I think of the remnants of a cigarette which literally blow away if subjected to the wind. Cremated human remains are more the consistency of sand; very granular and a bit heavier.

When a cremation is finished and the retort (oven) is cool enough to be opened, all that is left is a pile of bones...the only non-combustible part of the human anatomy. Depending on how the body was clothed, also included will be metal snaps, hooks or zippers, possibly a watch or a necklace, and certainly artificial knees, hips and other surgically implanted devices. If the decedent had a pacemaker or defibrillator, it would have been removed by the embalmer. These devices would explode during the cremation and could damage the equipment. The bones and other items are then raked into an "ash-pan" and poured onto the lid of a "processor." These items are separated from the bones via a powerful magnet and disposed of unless the director is told otherwise.

Once the operator is confident the only things left on the lid are skeletal human remains, the remains are swept into the processor. The lid is placed on the processor and the power is switched on. The processor runs for thirty seconds and presto, we have "ashes," or at least what you think are ashes. Obviously, these ashes have to be placed in some sort of a container.

Earlier in the book I told you about a "temporary container" and promised I would explain a little more about it. Well, here ya go. It's called a temporary container because it's inexpensive. It's a black or brown heavy plastic urn with a clear plastic liner (similar to a freezer bag). The word "temporary" implies that it isn't suitable for anything except to hold the ashes until a more expensive urn is chosen.

Before another urn is chosen, though, let's think about what you'll be doing with the ashes. Will it be placed on a mantel? If so, purchasing a more attractive urn would be appropriate. Will it be buried? If so, an "urn vault" might be required by the cemetery for the same reasons a casket vault might be required. If this is the case, there would be no reason to purchase anything other than the vault. Most would think it's silly to buy an expensive urn, only to be placed in a vault at the funeral home or crematory, never to be seen again. If a vault is not required, this "temporary urn" could be directly buried. It's durable enough to withstand the weight of 18 -24 inches of dirt.

Wilbert Vault Company makes an urn called "The Tribute."It's made of a marbelon material, is pretty enough to be displayed on a shelf, and is durable enough to be buried without a vault. Most cemeteries would accept this urn without the need to purchase an urn vault. So if you want something more than the plastic box urn but don't want to spend a lot, this is an excellent choice. I sell this urn for $150.

I recently handled the cremation and memorial service of a 53-year old man named Stephen. His 81 year old father chose to make his urn. It was a "double-wide", with a space for Stephen's wife, who will be cremated after her death. This is perfectly acceptable. He did a marvelous job, beautifully handcrafted and made with the same care and compassion I used when embalming my father.

Just like caskets, you'll see a variety of urns. And just like the caskets, you'll see the urns they hope you'll buy. But again, there are many more choices in the catalogs the funeral homes carry. If the funeral home doesn't carry the style of urn you like or doesn't have one in your price range, peruse these catalogs.

When one thinks of an urn, the picture that comes to mind is a vase. It will have a "curvy" figure with a fancy lid. The truth is this is only one kind of urn. The alternatives include everything from a wooden chest to a brass cube, a clock to a bronze dolphin, or a porcelain urn with a religious theme to a bio-degradable urn made from earthen clay. We even carry "memento urns," or "keepsakes," which allow us to place a minute amount of cremated remains in separate, much smaller urns for distribution to several different loved ones. "So many choices, so little time..." Oh how untrue!

Cremation affords you the time to make decisions. Decide what you want *after* you know what you need.

Chapter 11

Cash Advances

I've been to so many seminars through the years sponsored by consultants who make their living telling us, as funeral home owners, what we're doing wrong. We are so focused on "service" that we forget at what cost. "You've created this monster," they'll say. And they're correct. "If my competitor pays for the funeral luncheon and has to wait 30-60 days to get paid, well, by God, I will too!" At least the restaurant got their money today. "If my competitor pays the $1000 grave-opening fee and has to wait 30-60 days to get paid, by God, I will too!" At least the cemetery got their money today. Meanwhile, the families we serve think we're the greatest thing since sliced bread.

Most families do pay within 30-60 days. Some families pay sooner and, hallelujah, some pay immediately! But guess what…some don't pay at all. Yet, the restaurant and the cemetery, the minister, musician, the hairdresser, and the newspapers got paid today...by the funeral home.

And don't forget about the vault or concrete box installation fee. This was discussed briefly awhile back. It really should be treated as a cash advance so you won't have to pay sales tax. If this fee is included in the price of the vault, ask the funeral director to separate this charge so the tax is less, unless of course your state taxes for "services rendered."

The obituary published in the newspaper is a cash advance with a cost you can sometimes control. I say "sometimes" because the longer the obit, the higher the cost, obviously. This is particularly true with newspapers in large, metropolitan areas. Smaller towns, however, sometimes have a set fee — often as little as $25 no matter the length — while other small towns don't charge at all.

Our hometown newspaper, *The Edwardsville Intelligencer*, recently started charging out of town funeral homes $50 for an obituary. The three Edwardsville funeral homes were not charged originally. This fee was implemented because one of our neighboring funeral homes had a habit of writing obituaries which were at least twice the length of the standard obits. Included would be the complete life history of when and where the person lived, worked, and dined; the name of every child, grandchild, great-grandchild, niece, nephew, aunt, uncle, close friend, and pet; his work history which would rival the best resume ever written; and his favorite song, poem, hobby, book, author, and color.

When the newspaper started to charge for these obits, the owner of this funeral home called me and asked, "Why are they charging us for obits and not you?" I said, "Because you're writing a biography instead of an obit." In those days, obits were faxed and someone in the newsroom had to actually retype the copy. Now everything is emailed, copied, and pasted, but it still takes up a lot of space.

When going over the obituary information with your funeral director, ask which papers charge and how much...because the fees will definitely vary. An obituary can easily be edited to a reasonable length. For example, if it is submitted to the *Chicago Tribune* because the person lived there 40 years ago, there would be no need to list the names of all the survivors or the person's work history. His old friends in Chicago don't need to know that he was a member of the Edwardsville Senior Citizens Center or a 4th Degree Knight of Columbus. What they need to know is to whom he was born, where he lived in Chicago and what other connections to the city he had.

It takes just a few words to make a "column inch," which is how the newspapers charge, so be selective in what you say and to which papers. The *St. Louis Post Dispatch* charges $30 for a simple death notice. All it includes is the person's name, the town in which they lived, and the service information. An average size obituary is $250 minimum. Have the funeral director edit these obits as needed and make sure he gets confirmation of the exact charges before approval. If you're not careful, you could easily have $500 worth of newspaper notices. Some of this may be unnecessary, especially in the days of the internet. Almost every funeral home by now has a website and, if so, these obits will be listed for free.

All cemeteries have a "grave opening and closing" fee. This, of course, is the cost to dig the grave and fill it back in after the burial. This charge varies greatly, but is usually never cheap. A small rural cemetery might still dig the grave by hand (seriously) and only charge $225, while the large privately owned cemetery uses a backhoe and charges $1200. You might think, '$1200? It only took him 20 minutes.' True, but the cost to run the backhoe, insure it, pay the operator, etc., is not a small expense. Cemeteries and gravediggers have overhead just like funeral homes.

Remember my story about Earl, the gravedigger? He was an absolute magician with that backhoe, but it came at a price. After all, I couldn't jump in there and do it. I had a burial at a local cemetery which was known for its hills, and this particular winter morning the grave was located near the bottom. There was no way I was going to get my hearse near the grave with all of the snow and ice. Earl said, "Put it in my bucket. I'll get it down there." I was a bit reluctant, but I trusted his judgment. Earl got that hardwood casket down to the grave without a scratch. At the time, the grave opening fee was $600. I'd say it was worth every penny.

Some years ago, I had a burial near Ottumwa, Iowa, the fictional home of Corporal Radar O'Reilly from the M*A*S*H television series. Since it was about a 6-hour drive, I drove there the day before. A good funeral director always makes a dry run to an unfamiliar cemetery. When we are leading a funeral procession, our biggest fear is making a wrong turn. I know of one funeral director who didn't make that dry run, and not only did he make the wrong turn, but he led the procession to a dead end (no pun intended). Thirty cars had to stop, turn around, and start over. That's almost as embarrassing as getting to the cemetery and realizing you forgot to order the vault.

At any rate, this burial in Ottumwa didn't require a procession, but I did need to know where it was to ensure that I would arrive prior to the family on the day of the burial. Upon my arrival at the cemetery the day before, I noticed a gentleman sitting in his truck eating an apple. Meanwhile, an elderly woman was in the grave with a shovel. The gravedigger's name was Williams. I asked the gentleman in the truck, "Should I have written this check to Mrs. Williams?" He said, "She's a fine woman." I wonder if Mrs. Williams thought $400 was enough.

People ask me all the time what a minister should be paid to conduct a funeral. It will vary from nothing to a couple hundred dollars. It just depends on the minister and the situation. I usually give the minister a minimum of a hundred dollars. Some would argue that Mom or Dad gave to the church every Sunday for the last 50 years so the minister should do it for nothing. Maybe, but this minister might have been there for only the last two years or so. Also, he or she is rearranging his or her schedule to accommodate the family and is probably putting in a great deal of time to prepare so the funeral is personalized. Most clergy like to meet with the family for a few hours a day or two before the funeral, especially if they don't know them well.

Although this is true in most cases, I've worked with clergy who didn't deserve anything. I remember one minister in particular. He would arrive at the service at 9:45, ask for an obituary, read it, ask me how to pronounce certain names, walk in at 10:00, and have the most generic funeral you'd ever witness. I always said that's the easiest 100 bucks anyone could make.

Musicians are another cash advance which will depend on the particular situation. Typically, musicians shouldn't be paid as much as the clergy, but they do deserve a generous stipend. Again, you might think, "A hundred dollars and all they did was play one song?" Yes, but let's think about this. I'll use my dad's funeral as an example. As stated early in this book, he was a musician, and my mom wanted "Danny Boy" played on the trumpet at his funeral. I contacted the music department of Southern Illinois University at Edwardsville. A man by the name of Mr. Anderson drove the 40 miles to the church and belted out a beautiful version of "Danny Boy" after communion. It was a tremendous gift to my mom and a wonderful tribute to my dad. He was paid $200, but it was probably worth more.

Cash advances are a convenience for the family. Because of our generosity, families don't have to write seven or eight checks and disperse them as needed the day of the funeral. Whatever the amount due the minister, musicians, hairdresser, etc., is the amount on the contract. If there is a charge for handling these fees, it must be noted. But typically there isn't.

I was taken aback once by a family who told me of the conversation they had with a particular sexton at a local cemetery. In addition to the grave opening and closing fees, this family had to actually purchase the grave space for a funeral to be held in the next few days. When asked about paying the cemetery, the sexton informed them, "If you don't want to pay now the funeral home can take care of it, and you can settle up with them." Needless to say, I had a talk with the sexton.

If I can't get paid within 30 days, I require my families to at least pay for the cash advances. It's only fair. That's money out of my checkbook. Once in awhile I'll have a family suggest paying this fee before I share my policy. When this happens, I know I'm dealing with a family that probably owns a business.

They understand.

Notes

_____

_____

_____

_____

_____

_____

_____

_____

_____

_____

_____

Chapter 12

"Pre-Need"

Back in the 1970s, arranging for your funeral ahead of the need came into vogue. It really wasn't started by the funeral homes, but rather by the folks who wanted to make sure their wishes were carried out and the burden lifted from their families. To this day, these are the two main reasons "pre-arrangements" are still being done. At least that's what the funeral homes want you to believe. Although these are truly legitimate reasons, funeral homes like pre-arrangements for financial reasons. "Clear your minds, lift the burden from your family, ensure your wishes are carried out, and give your money to me."

At some point, probably in the late 70s and early 80s, consumers started to pre-pay their funerals with the guarantee the price will be "locked in." We started to see the potential market for this, so insurance companies jumped in and said, "We'll fund it for you." Banks also said to the funeral home, "Bring your pre-need money to us and we'll set up a trust. You decide if it'll be a 16-month or a 12-month certificate of deposit. Just take the higher interest rate."

State laws were enacted so we became the "trustees," which allowed us to keep part of the principal and interest. In Illinois, for example, when depositing the money from the consumer, we can retain 5% of the original principal and 25% of the annual interest. These fees were due us because we maintain these accounts, make deposits for the consumer as needed, report to the Comptroller's Office annually, etc.

If you think this is excessive, let me tell you a story. Many years ago, a little lady from Edwardsville came to my office and wanted to pre-pay her cremation. At the time, the total bill would have been around $1200. She started with an initial deposit of $100 and wanted to pay $25 per month until her contract was fulfilled.

Every month on or around the third, I would get a $25 check in the mail from Evelyn, followed by a phone call from her asking, "Joe, did you get my check?"

"Yes, Evelyn, I did."

"Did you deposit it yet?" she'd ask.

"Not yet, Evelyn, but I'll get it there today."

After about two and a half years of these monthly trips to First Federal Savings and Loan in Edwardsville, and a grand total of about $950 with interest, I told her in her monthly call to me, "Evelyn, guess what? It's all paid. You don't owe any more."

"Really? I thought I had a little more to go."

"Nope. It's taken care of."

When she died, I was a little short, but she got just exactly as she wished and I thought of those 12 trips I *didn't* have to make to the bank.

Another little lady named Loretta never married. She was known to be worth several hundred thousand dollars, if not more. I can't count the times she came to me and said,

"Joe, I need to talk to you about my arrangements." Being a young owner and eager to do business with anyone, with or without money, I would anxiously reply, "Anytime, Loretta. Please give me a call."

After no less than a dozen of these exchanges over a three year period, (I told you I wasn't very good at this) I finally said, "Loretta, how about next Tuesday?" (Apparently I'd been to a recent sales seminar.) She said, "No. I don't think that will work. My nephew will be in town." After several other casual attempts, I finally decided Loretta did not want to let go of her money, not even for her own funeral — which is precisely why she had the money she did.

Loretta died a few years later. I handled her funeral and was paid quickly by her estate. I placed her in a **simple** 20 gauge steel casket and the Monticello vault. If you remember, the Monticello is **simple**, but very good. It was a very **simple** funeral; just a few friends and family with everything completed in about 3 hours. The burial was in a **simple** country cemetery on a beautiful summer morning. The only thing not simple was her willingness to pre-pay while alive. So you see, the fees we collect can also make up for the fees we'll never collect despite our efforts.

I recently sold a piece of rental property through a real estate agent. Two weeks after the listing began, we were offered $2000 less than the asking price, in cash, and "Let's close next week." Based on the $147,000 sales price, my agent's commission, which was split with her agency, was a cool $8820. She was a bit embarrassed her commission came so easily. I told her not to worry about it. It makes up for all the times she works her tail off and gets next to nothing. I hired her to do a job and she did it, so who am I to complain?

When pre-arranged funerals are funded through a life insurance policy, commissions are paid to the funeral home. This, of course, is another incentive for the funeral home to seek pre-arrangements. The younger the person or the healthier, for example, the higher the commission will be. There's nothing wrong with this. After all, the funeral home has expenses in providing this service. Someone must have a license to sell life insurance, there's time involved, etc. But don't think for a minute when a funeral home seeks your pre-arrangement they're doing it strictly for your benefit. It has to be of benefit to them as well.

I have never been a big fan of pre-paid funerals. Mostly, though, I have never been a big fan of *soliciting* pre-paid funerals. Again, I'm a terrible salesperson. And in order to increase my pre-need base I have to make "cold calls," follow up on leads, be persistent, and accept rejection. For me, accepting rejection is the easy part. When I was a younger funeral home owner, I had competition that was aggressive with pre-need. I felt I had to do it, even though it wasn't fun. When someone came to me, I was fine. "Please, sit down. I'll help you in any way I can." And I would take the time to do it. I didn't have to ask them to do it. I didn't have to call them repeatedly until they were tired of me. I didn't have to "close the deal." They *wanted* to pre-pay their funerals.

Funeral homes will guarantee or "lock in" the price of a funeral at today's price. As long as the same services and merchandise are selected at the time of death, you'll pay nothing more than the contracted price, even if the death occurs many years from the date of the contract. The risk is on the funeral home, not the consumer. This is another reason I have never been a fan of pre-paid funerals. Cash advances should not be guaranteed because they are charges not controlled by the funeral home. I've seen funeral homes guarantee cash advances and get burned at the time of death. If a person pre-paid $1400 for the grave opening, obituary notices, death certificates, etc., and two years later those items totaled $1900 because of increases we don't control, there's a good chance we'll be short. That's not the consumer's problem, it's our problem. So chances are, you'll see these items listed as "non-guaranteed cash advance items." If so, you may be liable for increases at the time of death.

If you're disciplined enough, you could do just as well by creating your own savings account for your funeral. I know you might think, "Well, Joe, I can lock in today's prices by setting it up with you." True, but we keep the interest. That's the only way we can guarantee the funeral costs. With your own account, you're simply turning the interest over to us at the time of death, which offsets the inflation. So it's your choice. You can give us the principal and we'll maintain it or you can do it yourself. Make the deposit and let it go. It's a lot easier for you to do it than it is for us. But you have to be disciplined enough not only to do it, but to save it also.

I have given you reasons why some folks choose to pre-pay. There is another one, however, and it's important to discuss. I'm talking about "spend-down" situations. If a person is in a nursing home and their care is being paid with the individual's own money, it's quite likely that money will be exhausted before the person dies. Nursing care is not cheap. $3000 per month is on the low side. If one is not independently wealthy, he or she will outlive the money. Many states will allow that person to "spend-down" by pre-paying their funeral. All of their assets must be exhausted before state aid eligibility. No house, cars, life insurance cash value or other assets are allowed. A person may have a limited amount of cash necessary for "daily living." In Illinois it's not to exceed $2000. This fund can be used for things such as clothing and a weekly hairdresser.

Funeral expenses or "final expenses" are inevitable. So our state allows one to pre-pay. All merchandise is exempt from state aid. These items can include, but are not limited to, the casket, vault, urn, flowers, grave space, head stone, engraving, register book, and all printed material.

Services such as transportation from the place of death, automobiles, facilities, and embalming are exempt up to a certain amount, probably in the neighborhood of $4500.

Let's say Grandma sold her house and moved to a nursing home three years ago. She is down to about $20,000 after having paid for her care with the proceeds of the sale. She, or her Power of Attorney, can elect at this time to pay for her funeral. She could spend $10,000 on some of the merchandise mentioned in the above paragraph, $4500 on services and have $5500 left over. This money will be used to pay for another month and a half of nursing care and the rest can be left in her personal account. Or she could spend $5000 on the merchandise, $3000 on services and $12,000 would remain to pay for her care. The more you pay for the funeral, the sooner the state aid kicks in. In a situation like this, we would set up a "guaranteed trust" and have it "irrevocably assigned" to the funeral home. This means the money used can only be spent on her final expenses. It cannot be withdrawn and used for anything else.

At the time of death, if the money in the trust does not cover the current prices, we have to accept the loss. Consequently, any money left over does not have to be refunded. If the decedent was on state assistance, any excess funds have to be spent on the funeral in the form of a more expensive casket, another limo, additional flowers, etc., or the money goes back to the state. It cannot be refunded to the family or any other beneficiaries.

Funeral homes love this. If they see that the fund has grown substantially, they start thinking, "We'll move her up to a copper." But it's up to you. Do you give it to the funeral home or give it back to the state? I can see both scenarios. Your local funeral director is a nice guy and he has kids to feed, but the state did care for Grandma for the last couple of years. Although here in Illinois, the citizens have been victim to such corrupt leadership that one might think, "Screw the state. Let's put Grandma in that copper."

If you decide to pre-pay for your funeral, ask how it will be funded. The risk is always on the funeral home, but make certain you know if it's a trust—guaranteed or non-guaranteed—or an insurance policy for burial. It's just prudent for you, as a consumer, to know.

There was an insurance company from Missouri which funded pre-paid funerals for funeral homes in

Missouri, Illinois, and Texas. It's too complicated to explain what illicit activity led to its downfall, but suffice it to say they are no longer in business. And when a funeral home has to provide the services and merchandise which were guaranteed, they're lucky to get back the original premium. This company has been in the news a lot lately and I've taken many calls from concerned consumers. Fortunately, I've had very few contracts with them; but I know of colleagues who've invested millions, and it's a shame.

Many other funeral homes have fallen victim to a state association which I will not name. When the little lady from small town, USA came in to pre-pay her funeral, the funeral home sent her money to the state association and a trust was set up. Because this state association was overseen by a board of unpaid funeral directors who had no expertise in financial investments, the two or three people at the top had a little too much power and got a little greedy. Consequently, this state association is facing a 40 million dollar deficit.

Let's say this lady pre-paid in 1995 and the cost of her funeral at the time was $6000. This lady died in March of 2010. The cost of this same funeral was now $12,000. The funeral home received a check from the state association for $5500. That's a $6500 loss. What an investment. The lady got her funeral, but the funeral home took a huge hit. I know of funeral homes that are accepting losses to the tune of 100 grand per year because of this debacle. Although the consumer is protected, you must beware. Situations like this can bankrupt a firm, and then *you* would have the problem.

Although I've indicated I'm not a big fan of pre-need, it does provide peace of mind. Your wishes will be carried out and the burden of arranging will be lifted from your survivors. Your personal history and death certificate information will be provided by you, not a child or grandchild who has no idea what your mother's maiden name was, what year you retired, or the proper name of the sorority in which you've been a member for 50 years.

If you are not ready to pre-pay for your final expenses, it's still not a bad idea to pre-arrange. Any funeral provider will be happy to sit down with you and explain all of your planning options. There typically isn't a "consultation fee" as there would be for a lawyer or accountant, and if you wish to pre-pay later you can always do so. While you should keep in mind that the prices never go down, don't let that be the deciding factor. Most funeral homes have only one price increase per year. If finances are discussed, ask how long the price will be in effect. Their fiscal year may be different than the calendar year; and in a pre-need situation they may be willing to honor the original cost even if they've had an increase. It will depend on your age, health, etc. It doesn't hurt to ask.

But there isn't much bargaining in the funeral business, and there shouldn't be. Our prices are what they are for a reason. Like any other retail or service oriented business, our cost of goods and services rises annually. Also, a deal to you is unfair to the family last week who had to pay the full price. But with pre-need the funeral home has time on their side, and this could work in your favor. You won't get a huge break but it could save you a couple hundred dollars.

Notes

_____

_____

_____

_____

_____

_____

_____

_____

_____

Chapter 13

I Love Cremation

Funeral home owners grumble the most when they have a garage full of expensive cars, a staff with little to do, and property taxes on a 7000 square foot building, all the while working with a 33% cremation rate. The grumbling can be just as loud from casket manufacturers for obvious reasons. So casket companies decided to start selling urns. They also started teaching funeral homes how to make money selling cremations.

When a funeral director hears "the 'c' word," he immediately thinks, "direct." Casket and urn manufacturers encourage us not to assume cremation to be cheap with no type of funeral service. So now, even though cremation might be the ultimate form of disposition 33% of the time, these families are given the choice of viewing prior to cremation, either private or public because viewing provides "closure." It's part of the grieving process and necessary for healing.

Do you remember my fictional story of the man who died in the emergency room? Well, in a case like that, I feel final viewing would be good for the bereaved. I do believe viewing the deceased helps one to experience the finality of death, which is important in the grieving process. However, don't let the funeral home talk you into it if you are truly comfortable without it. With viewing, embalming, other preparation of body and hairdressing may be necessary. Also a rental casket to the tune of $1500 or a cremation casket, ranging in price from $500-$2100 could also be required. So this viewing, which may or may not be necessary for you personally, will add another $2000 or more to the bill. Make sure it's right for you.

When arranging a cremation, you'll have more choices than what you would have ever thought. By law, the body has to be placed in some sort of cremation container. This doesn't mean a casket. It can be as simple as a cardboard box, but we can't put *just* a body in the cremation chamber. There are two reasons for this: crematory operators don't have to be licensed funeral directors or embalmers. They are sometimes not trained to handle deceased human bodies and the problems which they present. Also, unless the body is in a container, there would be no dignified way for the body to enter that chamber. It would have to literally be thrown in. We obviously would never do that.

In the old days, funeral directors wouldn't give you a choice. They simply assumed you'd want the minimum container. And if they charged enough, which most had done, they didn't care. But today, this will be explained to you. Which container or casket will you select? I don't advocate just the cardboard box. I also don't discourage it. If you are to have a private or public viewing, you may want to select something a little more dignified. You'll find a cremation casket that looks nice for well under $1000. And if you think it looks so much cheaper than an expensive casket, well, it is. But remember what you're there to do. This is not a traditional funeral so why go to that expense? You're being totally respectful even though you're selecting something much less expensive.

117

For those of you who feel viewing is not necessary, I hope you're right. You probably are, but there's no turning back. Cremation is irreversible. But if it is right for you, the minimum cardboard container is adequate. It will retail for under $100 and is usually sturdy enough to get the job done with dignity. If a person is 250 pounds or more, however, something sturdier may be necessary. The crematory operator doesn't want any accidents. Many cremation caskets, starting in the neighborhood of $500 are strong enough to hold 500 pounds.

The reason I chose the title of this chapter "I Love Cremation" is because, typically, cremation, especially direct cremation, is much less labor intensive for the funeral director. When my phone rings in the middle of the night while I'm experiencing the REM phase of my sleep, I get up and go. If the death occurs at a residence or a nursing home, they usually want the body out of there ASAP. And if embalming is requested, I do it immediately. People always ask me why. There are two reasons: most importantly, the sooner it's completed, the better the result. If embalming is done several hours after death, the blood becomes more viscous, drainage is more challenging, and distribution of fluid is not as thorough. Secondly, I like to stay ahead of myself. One never knows how busy the day may become. Having the embalming completed sooner frees up more time later.

Every year I speak to our local high school students who participate in the Medical Careers classes at Edwardsville High School. They always ask, "What's the worst part about being a funeral director?" The answer for me is easy: getting up and going to work in the middle of the night. I've been doing it for 22 years and have never gotten used to it.

So if I recognize the name of the deceased and I know it will be a cremation with no viewing, the first thing I think of is "Good. I can go back to bed at a decent hour. All I have to do is the removal." If this person dies at a hospital with a morgue, I don't even have to leave. I can go in the morning. This is good if you're more concerned about sleep than money. Money does concern me, but I *love* my sleep.

Another reason I love cremation from a business point of view is the manner in which our paperwork is filed. One of the only things the State of Illinois got right in recent years was our "Illinois Vital Records System" (IVRS). You see, we used to have to employ our local retired friends to deliver the death certificate to the doctor for signature. Our retired friend would sometimes sit in the Doctor's office for two hours and read magazines while waiting for the return of the signed certificate. Then he would trek off to the coroner's office to receive the "Coroner's Permit to Cremate." After this was done, he would drive over to the local registrar where the death certificate would be filed, certified, and copied and the final permit for disposition issued. All of this was done with our car, using our gas, and while paying him $10 an hour.

Now everything is done electronically. What my retired friend accomplished in four hours while driving a total of 35 miles, I can accomplish without leaving my office. Just the other day I dealt with two doctors, two coroners' offices, and two local registrars starting at 1:00 in the afternoon. By 5 p.m. all of my paperwork was completed and I paid no one but myself. And I did it all from the air-conditioned comfort of my own office.

This leads me to my next goal. It's a goal completely opposite of what every other funeral home in the nation would want: I want to do 150 cremations a year and 30 casketed funerals. That's 180 calls per year, and I can do it with very little extra help. I am on my way. My charge for direct cremation is $985. My average casketed funeral is $5000.

Most funeral homes would love 150 casketed funerals with only 30 cremations. Not me. But I didn't build the typical funeral home. I built a "practical" funeral home. *And this practical funeral home saves people a lot of money.*

Notes

_____

_____

_____

_____

_____

_____

_____

_____

_____

_____

_____

Chapter 14

🍁

Making a Change

Most funeral homes are 6,000–8,000 square feet in size and have off-street parking for 50 cars or more. The typical funeral home will also own a fleet of late model Cadillacs or Lincolns. A new hearse is around $70,000. A new nine-passenger limo could be $50,000. A new Cadillac sedan is about $40,000, and the vans needed for removals and flower deliveries after the funeral are about $35,000 apiece. Every time I see a story regarding the funeral industry on *Dateline* or *60 Minutes,* I see us portrayed as money hungry vultures waiting for the next death so we can take advantage of the alleged vulnerability I described in the beginning of this book. According to them, we must be making a pile of money so we can drive those fancy cars.

The fact is, however, there is still a notable demand for full-service traditional funerals—an expected part of the tradition being the procession with those precise vehicles. And as long as there is, such funeral homes need to exist. Think about it. If Mom's wishes were to be buried just as the generations before her, with an evening visitation and a church service, would her children take her to a funeral home that's rundown and has rusty cars? I think not. I've seen funeral homes lose calls because the handicap ramp was too steep, the chapel was too small, the carpet was too old or there wasn't enough parking. If a traditional funeral home is to survive, it must spend money on cars and facilities.

The percentage of Americans being cremated rises annually. In 7 years the national average could easily be 50%. And boy, are the funeral homes grumbling. The typical funeral home will employ two licensed funeral directors and embalmers and employ part-time staff as well. All of this depends on the amount of volume a firm does, of course, but a rule of thumb is for every 50 calls you need one licensee. I once owned a firm with a "cursed" volume. On a good year I did about 80 calls. On an average year I did about 65. This means I was plenty big to support me, but not big enough to support another licensee. I was on call 24/7 and began to hate my career. So I changed courses. I worked out a deal with one of my competitors where I was simply employed by the firm. That's right...I got a paycheck every two weeks and had three weeks worth of vacation every year. I bought a small boat, we traveled a bit, and built eight years' worth of memories I hope my daughters never forget. I don't think they will.

In addition to wanting more time with my family, I could see the industry changing. As the owner of the funeral home, I could envision those 65 calls going down to 50 because of two new funeral homes under construction; and I could see the average revenue per call decreasing because of cremation and other less traditional forms of services. So selling my business felt like the right thing to do.

I was finally able to travel to Mexico with my family and spend a week on the beach. We traveled to San Francisco, where I carried my daughter, Olivia, across the Golden Gate Bridge when she was too tired to finish the walk. Teaching my daughter, Kelsie, to water ski was great fun. My wife, Cheryl, and I are huge Charlie Daniels Band fans, and as a family would travel wherever we could whenever we could to see a concert, whether it was in nearby St. Louis or 800 miles away in Williamsburg, VA. During those eight years of employment we traveled to the Florida beaches no less than four times and Disney World once.

When I was a kid, I experienced one family vacation—to Arkansas for 3 days. I'm not complaining. With his job at General Motors and playing music on the weekends, Dad worked seven days a week and we didn't know any better. So I wanted my kids to experience more, and they have. Heck, because of the generosity of my brother-in-law, Lawrence, they've even been to New York City and Tokyo, Japan. They saw more of the world before their tenth birthday than I have to this day.

But was selling my business truly the right thing to do? From a family point of view: absolutely. From a business point of view: probably. I say "probably" because it's too soon to tell. You see, at age 47, I'm starting over. I jumped ship from the security and comfort of a no-pressure job as a funeral director and embalmer to that of a funeral home and cremation center owner in another town where I'm known by few.

My wife is a very good business woman but chooses not to be. She's burned out. In 1994, she started a daycare center in a strip mall in Edwardsville with $10,000 borrowed from her father. Two years later we built a 4,400 square foot building to accommodate her growing business. By 2004 and ten years' worth of headaches she was ready to sell everything. From that sale, and the sale of my funeral home, we had a pretty good nest egg established, bought some rental property, and paid off our $300,000 home three years ago. The market was climbing and I thought I could retire in about ten years.

I was wrong.

We all know what happened in 2008. What made the financial collapse even more gut-wrenching for me was that was about the time I started to think about building my own funeral and cremation business, with an emphasis on cremation and other less costly services. Do you keep the money in the market or do you get out before it hits bottom? Where is the bottom? I'm a chronic worrier anyway, so you can imagine the sleepless nights I experienced. Thank God for Dr. Michael Mulligan and Lexapro.

To make a long story short, we lost a lot but had just enough to make this next project possible. We had to mortgage our home a second time to do it and I felt blessed that, in this economy, we had a bank willing to work with us.

So here was my plan: I wanted to build a funeral home and crematory just big enough and efficient enough to provide funeral and cremation services, but at a reduced price. So I didn't need a 7,000 square foot building. I wasn't interested in having a chapel that seats 100 people. Forty was plenty. I didn't need a big garage because I intended to rent my funeral cars when needed. I didn't need space for a selection room because I wanted to sell caskets out of a book so I wouldn't have the inventory expense.

My bankers thought it sounded wonderful so they asked me why many others aren't doing the same. I was not prepared for that question but had no trouble answering immediately. Let's think about the people who would have the knowledge, the capital, the licenses, and the "cojones" to undertake such a project. Many funeral homes are passed down from generation to generation. Does a 40-50 year old funeral director who had the business given to him by his father really want to go out on a limb? No, because it's been easy for him. Why should he assume such a risk when his business is paid for, he's drawing a nice salary, and he can just coast? He might have the knowledge and the capital but not the interest or the passion. It is the exception rather than the rule, but many "sons" of the funeral business are lazy and depend on others to do the work. I've seen it over and over again.

There's also the young man or woman who has just graduated from mortuary school who truly has a passion for the business, not because he or she was raised in the funeral home, but because he or she developed a sincere desire to work in this business. This was me in 1988 upon my graduation from Worsham College of Mortuary Science in Chicago. I understood what a difference we can make in this industry. But in 1988, I certainly didn't have the capital or the experience to make such a project work.

So now let's talk about the cojones. If there are two things I've learned about business in the last 22 years it's this: You don't get anywhere unless you take risks and the only way you will develop any wealth is if you are the owner. I would much rather look back and say "I tried" instead of "what if?" But I'll never have to say, "*at least* I tried" because failure is not an option.

And while my goal in life is not to be independently wealthy, I do want to retire at a decent age so I can have at least 20 years of good health on the golf course near our future summer home. I've buried way too many people who didn't get to enjoy such a life. So I'm willing to assume this financial risk at my age. My conclusion to the bankers' question was this: I fit the mold. I have the knowledge, the capital, the licenses, and the guts to go for it. And I know there's a need. I'm convinced this is the direction in which the industry is headed. If we don't change with it, we'll be left in the dust.

Brian Jones and Dominic Seipp from TheBank of Edwardsville said, "Welcome aboard, Joe. We'll help you in any way we can."

Chapter 15

Just What I Need

My realtor, Terry Johnson, is pretty sharp. And he's a good listener. When I described what I was looking for, he put a picture in his head and went to work. Within two days he emailed me photos of Wilson Siding and Windows, a store which had been on the market for some time. It was a 40 x 80 wood frame building sitting on a half acre. It was built in 2000 and is located on a federal highway with a traffic count of 13,600 cars daily. There were other locations which were more desirable, but cost was a factor. Instead of paying $500,000 or more for this building in a business district, I paid $250,000. Although this property is zoned B-2, other nearby properties include light industrial, agriculture, and other businesses. Next door to the east is a well-kept single family home and to the west, an open field. Across the highway is a very attractive small building used by a satellite TV company. My building has white vinyl siding and, with the steep pitch of the roof, looks like a church without a steeple. Perfect.

Obviously, I had to convert the building from its former use to that of a funeral home and crematory. But I never intended to build a traditional funeral home. I wanted a building which would be practical. When giving tours of my new establishment, I always remind people that my building is just what I need and nothing more. I have a "gathering room" which comfortably seats 40 people. I have a small coffee lounge with ample cabinetry, a sink, water cooler, and refrigerator. Our building has two offices; one for me (the big one) and one for my wife.

Our selection room is small since we don't stock full size caskets. I sell them out of a catalog. I know of funeral homes that carry $50,000 worth of inventory, and it's not on consignment. Who do you think has to pay for that? It's part of the overhead I described earlier in this book. The only inventory I actually stock are my urns and a few register books — less than a $1,500 inventory investment.

The former 1,900 square foot garage in this building was converted into a one-car garage, an embalming room, and a crematory. That's right—my crematory is located onsite. Most funeral homes sub-contract their cremations since it's not practical to make that investment if you're the average funeral home. It was definitely an expensive part of my project but I decided it was worth it. This is my focus, and I'm playing for keeps. I only wish I could have afforded a pet crematory as well. I'm convinced many people will spend more on the death of their pet than their spouse.

I almost forgot to mention our restrooms. Since our building was built on a concrete slab and only nine years old when it was purchased, it was already very much handicap accessible. According to local codes, we had to add a urinal in the men's room. With the construction, we obviously had to repaint and install new flooring.

Also, according to the O'Fallon, Illinois building codes, our building became classified as "an assembly" because of the intended use as a funeral home and its ability to occupy 54 people, according to the square footage. For this reason, all of the heating, ventilation, and air conditioning had to be upgraded. The city also enforced other codes such as minimum parking standards, green space, paving, vinyl fencing, curbs and gutters, etc. You might think "what a pain they must've been." Not really. They were just doing their job and had the best interest of the city at heart. I'm okay with that. After all, I was a new business owner in their community who had a good reputation in my former town. I certainly didn't want to ruffle any feathers. And now that the project is completed, I have a lovely building on a beautiful piece of property. I'm proud of it and the city has been most gracious with me. We got off to a great start and I intend to keep it that way.

So, what's the key to my future success? Keeping my overhead low without sacrificing quality service and modern facilities. Let's talk about quality service.

I won't profess to be God's gift to the art and science of embalming, but when it comes to service I'll put myself up against anyone. When I was in mortuary school, I had a classmate who tried desperately to impress every teacher. He would ask questions when he knew the answers and always strived for one on one time with the instructor. You know the kind. We just rolled our eyes and said he's probably going to make a good funeral director because he's such a good ass-kisser. At the time, that's what we thought a good funeral director had to be.

Thankfully, we were wrong.

When it comes to serving a family I have one rule for me and anyone who works with me; give them what they need and get out of their way. I didn't learn that in mortuary school and I didn't learn it from any mentors of mine. I learned it on my own, working for myself, and it became my style. I believe you can kill a person with kindness. Early in my career a man died in his home. I responded to the call and while at the house his widow gave me instructions on the simplicity of their wishes. I sensed that about the only thing this family needed from me was to get the obituary published, get the death certificates, and get Dad cremated. Done. When I delivered the certified copies of the death certificate, she told me, "Joe, you were perfect." I said, "Excuse me?" She said, "We didn't need a lot from you and you didn't give it to us. You gave us the space we needed. Thank you." I suspect my former classmate wouldn't have done as well.

Other times you can't do enough. In 1997 I completed the addition of a handicap, unisex restroom on the main level of my 150-year old building which served as my "traditional" funeral home. An out-of-town family member, who just happened to work in Texas for Service Corporation International (SCI), the largest funeral home and cemetery conglomerate in the world, asked me where my lounge was. I pointed and told her "Down those steps." She asked, "You don't have an elevator?" Now, mind you, she had no problem with mobility. When I told her, "No, but I'll be happy to get you a cup of coffee and bring it to you," she smugly said, "No. That's alright. I just thought you'd have an elevator." I had just spent 20 grand on a toilet and she's complaining about having no elevator to use. Somewhere in between these two families is the norm.

When it comes to doing well in a service-oriented business, one has to be a good listener, just like my realtor was—and when it comes to making funeral arrangements, good listening skills are a must. Someone once said, "We have two ears and only one mouth, so listen twice as much as you talk." I know of some funeral directors who talk just to hear themselves talk. When asked a question, they give a definite answer whether it's correct or not. I believe credibility goes a lot further if you can just say, "I don't know, but I will find out."

I'll admit that I'm not the greatest listener at home. My wife will attest to that. I will even ask her, "Did I already ask you that question?" She'll say "Yes you did." So when she complains about me not listening to her I'll say, "See. I don't even listen to myself talk." I think I listen so well to the families I serve that I neglect to listen well at home.

Now that we've discussed quality service, let's talk about modern facilities. Does modern facilities mean big and expensive? No. It means clean, accessible, and practical. I've tried very hard to have my building reflect the attitudes of today's consumer. If simple is what you want, simple is what you'll get. I'm sure you'd like professional treatment, so you'll get that, too. And it won't cost extra. If you request embalming, I can do it. If it's a private service with 40 people or less, you'll be comfortable. If cremation is your choice, it will be done and I'll be the only one involved from start to finish. If you want a memorial service after the cremation but don't need me to be there, I won't. But I'll print a register book and memorial folders for you. It will only be an extra

$75 and you'll have a nice remembrance of the day. If it's a big funeral and you expect a couple hundred people or more, let's use your church. The price is the same.

If you want a direct cremation with no service you need a funeral director, not a funeral home. I've read about some funeral directors who actually work out of their home, with their only equipment being a van and a cot (gurney). I feel this is taking *simple* to the extreme. Although the consumer will get by cheaply, you'll not get the customer service to which you're entitled. I am somewhere in between. I do have overhead expenses, but not like the average funeral home. I can't get by as cheap as the guy in the van, but you will save money using my services.

So instead of a multi-million dollar investment, I have closer to $650,000 in this project; both borrowed money and my own cash. Is this too much? I originally thought I'd get by for much less but, like all major projects, some unforeseen challenges popped up. I'm confident it isn't too much. This is where the industry is headed and I want to be there when it arrives.

In the St. Louis, Missouri metro area, building a new funeral home would cost one and a half to two million dollars; and a rule of thumb in our industry is if you have two million dollars in your funeral home, you had better do 100 calls per year. It would be best to hope for 100 "casketed adult funerals," but in reality it won't be. Most likely it will be 60 casketed adult funerals, 33 cremations with or without a service, two immediate burials, three anatomical donations, and two infant deaths. Unless you're relocating your existing business or are in an area in dire need of a traditional home, I honestly can't understand why anyone would want to do it.

Let's say the bid to build it is $1,500,000. With a commercial loan at 6%, you'll pay $90,000 per year in interest alone. Property taxes will vary but could easily be $25,000 per year. And let's not forget about the principal payment, salaries, insurance, utilities, vehicles, and other expenses. You get the idea. I want my business paid for in five to ten years, and I don't want to have to sell $15,000 funerals to do it. I feel I can pay for it in five to ten by selling $1,000-$5,000 services, but I'll need volume. It's the Wal-Mart philosophy; sell it for less but sell more of it.

After eight months in business, I have already done 20 calls. This may not seem like much, but it's not uncommon for new funeral homes to do less than five calls their first year. Twenty calls are not enough, obviously, and I'm still not making money. Nor did I expect to by this time. But I'm on pace to do 25-30 calls this year. I'm confident that number will double in 2011; in 2012 even more, and on and on. I also have 14 pre-paid funerals on the books. People know I am here and they like what I am doing. Yes, my family and I are still hungry but we've adjusted. We just keep saying our prayers and constantly promote this business, whether it's paid ads on the obit page or walking around church picnics with our logoed shirts. It will happen, hopefully sooner rather than later. I don't want to have to wait five years to get to a comfortable volume, so I have another plan.

Chapter 16

"Will You Join Me?"

When I was making the trip to Chicago every month in 1987-88 while in mortuary school, I drove by many small towns along Interstate 55. You'll notice I said "by" and not "through" because the interstate has taken us away from small town America—which is precisely why these towns have nothing more than a church, two taverns, and a population of 900. Travelers go by them and not through them anymore. Interstate 55 between St. Louis and Chicago is pretty much the old Route 66. Historic Route 66—the highway made famous in song and in writing. My first funeral home, on St. Louis Street in Edwardsville, Illinois, was located on Route 66, right in the heart of town, with Tanyard Hill to the south and Mooney Hill to the north. Our town has its annual Route 66 Festival, a joyous occasion complete with food, drink, memorabilia, and classic cars.

For those of us too young to remember traveling the famed highway, all we can do is listen to stories and look at pictures. We imagine the family traveling on vacation, stopping at "Dog 'n Suds" for a hot dog and a root beer, just before refueling at "Jack's 66 Service Station." You remember...that's the place where Jack would actually come out and welcome you to town, ask where you're headed, check the pressure in your tires, the oil in your engine, clean your windshield, and offer you a safe trip as you leave. Most towns along this route have the preserved history of Route 66. But that's all it is now...history.

These towns are usually served by one or two funeral homes that simply have a branch in these towns, their main office in a larger neighboring municipality. If a town has a population of 900, it's probably an older population; and the older the population, the more deaths will occur. But in a town of 900, the average number of deaths per year will be around 15.

The funeral homes which serve these communities do not build new funeral homes. It is usually a house converted into a funeral home. State law says we have to have an embalming facility in each location, so any room with running water will be considered the embalming room. The chapel or the viewing room will be the former living room or parlor, and the lounge is what used to be the kitchen.

Parking is another situation. There almost never is a parking lot making street parking the norm. Not being restricted by the more stringent codes of the suburbs, the small town funeral home can get by more easily. It's not always convenient, but they get by nonetheless. So it isn't practical to build a new facility for a total volume of 15 funerals (or death calls that don't result in a funeral). Funeral homes want a branch in these small towns just so they get the calls. They would rather have a small investment in the community than concede the calls to a competitor.

In a way, these funeral homes are a throwback to yesteryear, not unlike Route 66 and the small town charm it embodies. But just as the interstate has changed these towns and the roads through them, the personal computer and the internet will continue to drastically affect these funeral homes and the industry in general.

As a business person, it obviously isn't prudent to build a two million dollar funeral home in a town which has 15 deaths per year. The "old Westmoreland home on Main Street" will suffice, especially since they put on that wooden ramp so a wheelchair can get in. "Besides," one might say, "I just want to be cremated. No visitation. Nothing. Just scatter my ashes in the lake where I used to fish." Let's not forget, of these 15 deaths per year, five of them will be cremated.

I have seen a tremendous increase in the attitude of keeping it simple. That's why cremation is on the rise. It's "simpler." No viewing, no fuss. And it's cheaper than a funeral. So if cremation is simpler, I want to go to the next level of simplicity...bringing the crematory to you.

The personal computer and the internet have changed us beyond belief. Just as electricity, the flush toilet, the automobile, and the airplane have made our lives more convenient, so has the PC and the World Wide Web. I know I'm having a slow day when I can't think of anything to search. The whole world is at our fingertips.

Welcome to my Cremation Society. It's in every town south of Springfield. Actually, it's in every home that has the Internet. It's perfect for those who wish for direct cremation. If convenience is what you want, convenience is what you'll get. You don't have to call for an appointment, drive here to meet me or tour my facility. All you need is a computer and the internet. You'll learn about my history and my family, including a link to Facebook where you can actually see pictures of us in our daily lives and photos of my funeral home and crematory. You can learn about embalming, if you wish, while taking a virtual tour of my preparation room. Whatever I want to share, it's yours. That's what the internet has done for us.

Earlier in the book I described how loyalty in this business is diminishing. Today's price-conscious consumer is looking for a deal. I handled the death of a gentleman last month whose wife was worried about the local funeral director, whom she's known for decades, not handling her husband's cremation. She explained to me that she and her husband were always somewhat frugal, always living within their means. I assured her they were not frugal. By living within their means, they were sensible. She felt somewhat guilty not calling her long-time friend/funeral director, but she saved $1,500.

With that in mind, I will bring my crematory to your town, and it will be located on your computer desk. It's a concept I did not invent, but it's one I'm excited about. It's called "Cremation Arrangement Websites." From the convenience of your own home, you can sit down at your desk, on your own time, and pre-arrange, pre-select, and pre-pay all of your services and merchandise. For those who prefer direct cremation with no service, you're in luck. You'll get it from me and you'll get it inexpensively, just like you want. My charge for this service is $1,150. If you become a member of my cremation society, that price will be reduced by $150. All it will cost you is a one-time $25 membership fee. The $150 savings is the main benefit, but don't forget about the convenience factor.

It's really quite simple. I need information for the death certificate and the obituary, which you will enter online. You can look at urns, all modestly priced, and select one with no pressure whatsoever. Remember the information I provided earlier about "thumbies" and other keepsake jewelry? You can peruse our online catalog and purchase your items as gifts for your grandchildren...and you'll be able to pay for everything online with the same safety and security as using PayPal.

If pre-paying is not an option, simply pre-arranging is acceptable. At least you'll have the "peace of mind" you hear so much about, of knowing your wishes will be carried out.

If you think I have a funeral home with lower overhead and operating expenses, you should see my cremation society. It's not a cheap website by any means, but it *is* just a website. And it's a way for me to expand my coverage area without brick and mortar. When building my funeral home and crematory, I put everything in place for this society, and at the time didn't even know it. I have the equipment, facility, licenses, knowledge, and experience to run this society. I just need the market...and a few billboards.

Notes

_____

_____

_____

_____

_____

_____

_____

_____

_____

_____

_____

Chapter 17

Conclusion

I still look at the obituaries every day. Every funeral home owner does. We need to see which funeral homes are busy and which ones are not. What's refreshing about my new business venture, though, is I don't have to worry when a competitor gets a call. You see, Instead of one or two competitors, I have many. And I'm in an area where not many know me personally. So how can I be offended if I don't get a certain death call. I'm simply trying to fulfill a need; a need for alternative types of funeral and cremation services. It's a need most funeral homes can't provide because of their business structure: high overhead, high prices.

I have many friends in this business, or at least so I thought, and quite honestly I haven't spoken to some of them since I opened my doors January 1, 2010. They've made no effort to call me, wish me luck, come over for a tour and a visit, or bring me a body which they need to have cremated. I guess in their eyes, I am now the enemy. Other funeral director friends (true friends) have called and wished me luck. To them I say "thank you." Some of them have stopped by just to see my place, and they've offered their compliments and admiration for what I am trying to do. They've expressed their understanding of what I am doing. These are the funeral directors who understand how our industry is changing.

Vendors are the same. I have seen very few of them since I opened my doors. I suspect some of them don't want their cars seen in my parking lot, for fear of another more lucrative funeral home customer driving by. Believe it or not, that's the way it is with some in this business. "If you sell to him, I'll never buy anything from you again." Unfortunate but true. Other vendors are very supportive and for that I am truly grateful.

They, like us, have never been afraid of change. We're also not afraid of failure. Even though failure is not an option, experiencing failure makes you grow. You learn from it. We've learned from past failures, so it's time to move on. One of my friends, Gary Bright, runs a very successful funeral business in Flora, Illinois. Anyone who has ever tried to compete with him has experienced failure. His success is due largely to his commitment to change. His is the only funeral home in town now, and he could very easily keep things static or become complacent. But he loves change. And so do the people of Flora, Illinois. As he once told me, "If you don't change with the times, you'll die on the vine." When they walk into his funeral home for a visitation, they see that he puts money back into his business with new wallpaper, carpet, furniture, and automobiles. He changes the casket companies he works with and other vendors also. Change keeps him interested, staying interested keeps him passionate about his business, and that passion creates his success. I've always admired someone with a passion for anything. Whether it's your business or hobby, having the passion to pursue it and be successful at it is an enviable trait.

My cremation society is not for everyone. Traditionalists will do things the way they've been done for years. My society doesn't work for them, and I can respect that. The people of Flora, Illinois know their funeral director is putting money back into his business, always keeping things fresh. They are also receiving value for their dollar, and that's extremely important. It's okay to spend a little more if there is value in your purchase.

"Value for your dollar"...that's a phrase I've used a lot the past 18 months. It's a great way to explain my business. Is $1,150 "cheap" for a cremation? Not if there's value in it. For that $1,150, you get professional and compassionate service from a licensed funeral director and embalmer. You get all of the necessary paperwork completed regarding the death, including assistance with VA forms, Social Security, and life insurance companies. You get dignified care and handling of the deceased in a modern and sterile environment. And ultimately, the cremation process is completed onsite by me, and me only. Would you say that's $1,150 well spent?...or $1,000 if you're a member of my society? And I can do it for that because I am embracing change and approaching my business differently than most.

One of my casket reps, Derrick Husmann, is also a licensed funeral director and embalmer. He did his apprenticeship under me years ago. He was then, and still is, a very energetic young man who is always thinking of change. What can we do that's different and creative to make ourselves and our businesses better? Two of my friends from the coffee shop I frequent in Edwardsville are former undertakers (which is a term I prefer over "morticians"), both graduates of mortuary school. Although Jeff Watson didn't continue his funeral career, he is a retired Professor of Anatomy from St. Louis University. Dale Nichols had many business interests after his funeral career, and even though he'd never admit it, has been very successful. What's common about these friends is not only their funeral service backgrounds, but their willingness to explore change, take chances, and pursue other interests. Their advice to me has been invaluable.

Change is inevitable. So get used to it. Some things change slowly, like the automobile and the airplane. Some things change quickly, like computers and cell phones. But make no mistake, changes will occur in everything eventually. For any funeral directors reading this book, you all know that porcelain embalming tables have been around for decades. Why? They never gave out mechanically. But now we have stainless steel tables with hydraulic adjustment pumps controlled by our feet. And they're better.

Some of us are changing not only our equipment but our entire methods of operation. We do so because you, the consumers, are changing. What's interesting to me, however, is you are compelling us to change while still being either misinformed or uninformed. Slowly, I think we are beginning to understand what it is you want. And, even more slowly, we are beginning to provide it.

The purpose of this book is to teach and inform you about the funeral and death-care industry—an industry which is oftentimes misunderstood. When I'm on an airplane and the passenger seated next to me finds out I am a funeral director, the rest of the flight is usually occupied by me answering question after question about what we do and why we do it. "Is it a state law? Why do you embalm immediately? How did you get into the business? How long does it take to cremate a body?"—and on and on and on. Do I mind? Not at all. I enjoy educating the consumer. Unlike the old days, I don't consider anything about this business to be "taboo." My doors are always open for a guided tour of my funeral home and crematory. You can get online and see it now.

I hope you've been enlightened. I hope you've been slightly entertained. But more importantly, I hope you've been educated. *You can afford to die!* Unlike not too many years ago, you have choices. Choices which fit your budget and beliefs — choices you have now because of your demands for us to change.

Change is good. Change is healthy. Routine is boring and makes us complacent. Change is refreshing and it keeps our minds healthy, always learning how to adapt. Succeeding is even more fun. And I'm not talking about succeeding just in business. My wife and I both come from small towns. We went to school, paid for college on our own, went to work in a new town where we started a new life. We became members of a new church, we shopped at new stores, and, more importantly, made new friends. These are friends we've been close to for over 20 years. That's what I call success. We could have stayed in our hometowns, comfortable with the way things were, never venturing out and taking a chance. Many people do, and that's okay. It's okay for some, but it wasn't for us.

We feel blessed and successful that we've been able to broaden our horizons by starting a new life 22 years ago. Our old life was quite good. We came from good families, grew up in nice towns, developed life-long relationships and had the stability we needed so that at age 18 we weren't afraid to "leave the nest" and make changes in our lives.

Without trying to invoke wisdom you don't need to hear, allow me to say that the measure of success is not how much money you have when you die or how many toys you've acquired in your life. Someone once reminded me that you never see a U-Haul truck following a hearse. Real success is being married to the right person, raising good children, having good friends, waking up happy, and enjoying hot fish and cold beer on a Friday night. Real success is not only laughing at a good joke, but also laughing at yourself. To be successful in life, you can't be afraid to say "I'm sorry" or "I love you." Success is when you see your child share her toys. Success is when your kids hug you and say, "You're the best dad in the world."

Everything else is gravy.

Key Points to Remember....

o Never feel pressured. If you are not comfortable with a certain funeral director, express it or ask to work with someone else. Remember funerals are for the *living*. You can respect the wishes of the dead and still do what's comfortable for *you*.

o Think about a budget, tell the funeral director what it is, and have him or her help you stay within it.

o The only "non-declinable" option is "Professional Services of Funeral Director and Staff". Everything else, from "Automobiles" to "Facilities" is declinable.

o Caskets: You can cut the cost of the casket in half if you request to see more choices. There are identical caskets made of different materials which look exactly the same.

o Vaults: Focus on the 3 *least* expensive. You will get what you need (or required by the cemetery) with any one of these.

o Out of town death: Call your funeral director back home. ***DO NOT* call a funeral home in the current location.** Your funeral director back home will sub-contract the necessary help needed to get the deceased home, and you will save $1500 - $2000.

o Other tasks dealing with the VA and Social Security should be handled by the funeral director. If assistance is needed in filing insurance claims, that is part of the funeral director's job also; don't be afraid to ask for help—and there should be no additional charges.

Appendix

Notes

_____

_____

_____

_____

_____

_____

_____

_____

_____

_____

Funeral Planning Checklist

For the obituary & death certificate, **g**ather necessary vital statistics, which would include

- name, address, date and place of birth; the names of the decedent's parents (including mother's maiden name).
- marital information, including the current marital status. You don't have to mention a divorce in the obituary, but the funeral director needs to know for the death certificate.
- the number of children, grandchildren, great-grandchildren; brothers, sisters, and other relatives.
- relatives who have preceded the decedent in death.
- educational background (i.e. the number of years education for the death certificate).
- work history, clubs, memberships, organizations (both community & professional).
- hobbies, interests, and other items you may feel are pertinent to your life.

- o social security number and veteran's history (if applicable, locate the DD 214, which is commonly known as "discharge papers").
- o the number of "certified" death certificates you'll need. This is dependent upon the financial situation and amount of assets there are, including the number of life insurance companies, number of car, truck, boat titles, etc., to be transferred; retirement accounts, and number of different financial institutions that need to be contacted.

If you are planning a burial

- o determine the type of service: Is it a traditional funeral with a viewing the evening before or the same day as service? Is it without a viewing, will it be a private or public service at the funeral home, your church, cemetery chapel or graveside – you have several choices.
- o what type of casket will you select? (hardwood or metal). Please refer to Chapter 7, "Merchandise, Caskets" for your review so you can make a "practical" decision.
- o what type of vault will you choose? Remember to ask your funeral director if one is required by the cemetery. If it is not a requirement, but you wish to purchase one, please refer to

Chapter 8, "Merchandise, Vaults" for another "practical" choice.

o a traditional service requires the following considerations: Times and locations of visitation and service; musical selections (usually CDs at the funeral home, an organist and/or vocalist at church are the most common options); floral tributes (a casket spray from the spouse and children is usually joined by a separate, but matching piece from the grandchildren).

o pallbearers will also be required. (Four to six is an ideal number but you may have eight. If you don't want to exclude anyone, consider "honorary pallbearers" who can line up behind the casket when processing.)

o clothing will need to be selected (again, refer to Chapter 9).

o a choice for the obituary should be made: to which papers, whether it is "free" or "paid"; remember to budget a certain amount and have the funeral director edit it as necessary.

If you are planning on cremation,

o will it be "immediate" or "direct", which means there is no service or viewing of any kind?

o will you have a cremation with a memorial service? (basically, a direct cremation but with a service; the body is not present) Will it be public or private without the presence of the deceased?

o are you choosing a traditional viewing and service where embalming is required for public viewing, followed by cremation? (Remember: a cremation casket or a "rental" would have to be selected.)

o you can opt for a private viewing for 1 hour (embalming is not required), followed by cremation.

o you can combine any of the above, followed by a graveside service in which the urn will be interred.

o select an urn which fits your needs: for burial, display on a shelf, stored in a closet or drawer (because it is uncomfortable to look at), etc.

When Pre-Paying

o ask how it will be funded; through a life insurance company or a trust.

o know the history of this life insurance company or trust organization. Have they been in business for decades or just a few short years?

o be aware of which parts of the contract are "guaranteed" and "non-guaranteed".

o ask if the contract is transferrable if the funeral home sells, goes out of business, or you decide to re-locate.

o will you receive correspondence from this company, the funeral home, or both, regarding the status of your agreement?

o what will be the financial consequences of changing plans? Will there be "administrative fees" in doing so? With an insurance-funded contract, what will the "cash value" be if canceled?

Notes

_____

_____

_____

_____

_____

_____

_____

_____

_____

_____

_____

Exhibit A:

Cost Analysis of a Traditional Funeral

Professional Services

Basic Services of Funeral Director & Staff	$1,795.00
Embalming	$595.00
Other Preparation of Body	$200.00

Facilities

Use of Facilities for Viewing/Visitation	$500.00
Use of Facilities for Funeral Ceremony	$500.00
Use of Facilities for Memorial Service	
Use of Equipment & Staff for Graveside Service	
Use of Equipment & Staff for Church Service	

Transportation

Transfer of Remains to Funeral Home	$225.00
Hearse	$200.00
Limousine	$200.00
Sedan/Lead Car	$185.00
Service/Utility Vehicle	
	$4,400.00

B Merchandise

Casket (or Other Receptacle)		$7,254.00
Name	Primrose Bronze	
Material	32 Ounce Bronze	
	Pink Velvet	
Color	Interior	

Outer Burial Container		$3250.00
Name	Bronze Triune	
	Concrete/Bronze	
Material	Liner	
Flowers		$300.00
Acknowledgement Cards		inc.

Appendix-Exhibit A: Cost Analysis of a Traditional Funeral

Register Book	$150.00
Memory Folders	inc.
Clothing	
Cremation Urn	
	$10,954.00

C Special Charges

Cash Advances

Death Certificates	$36.00
Clergy	$125.00
Musician	$100.00
Paid Obituaries	$550.00
Vault Co. Fee	$325.00
Tax	$869.00
Total	**$2,045.00**

TOTAL	**$17,399.00**

The preceding pages illustrate a "A Statement of Goods and Services". These are the previously described items which will appear on the funeral contract. Although not an everyday occurrence for most funeral homes, a $17,000 funeral will not surprise anyone these days. I have never sold a $17,000 funeral, but many funeral homes have, and continue to do so.

The "Service Charge" (A) in this case, is $4,400. If you remember, this is the charge which covers the funeral home's operating expenses, or overhead. This charge will vary from one funeral home to the next, obviously. But today, $4,400 is close to average, especially in larger markets. Also, if you'll remember from a few chapters back, the first charge listed, "Basic Services of Funeral Director and Staff", is the only *non-declinable* option. Everything else can be declined. We'll work on that in the next illustration.

Under "Merchandise" (B), you'll see a beautiful bronze casket, "The Primrose", by Batesville Casket Co.; a double-lined vault with a bronze liner, "The Bronze Triune", by Wilbert Vault Co.; and other merchandise such as printed material and flowers. This figure totals almost $11,000 and is taxable. The tax rate used is .0785, which is what I pay in St. Clair County, Illinois. In this case, it came to $869. We'll work on the merchandise also in the next illustration.

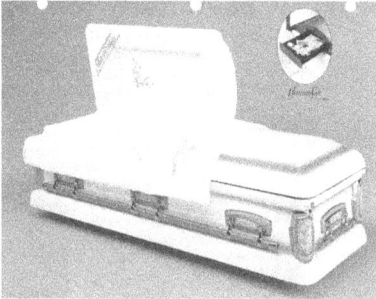

The cash advances (C) don't leave much room for adjusting. Again, these are the expenses paid by the funeral home as a "convenience" to the family. We'll do what we can to bring those down, but most of the cash advances are what they are.

No doubt this would be a lovely service. And with this kind of merchandise, every extra effort by the funeral director will be made to ensure your comfort and satisfaction. However, all reputable funeral homes should give you the same level of service, no matter what merchandise is sold.

What kind of life insurance do you have? $5,000, $10,000, $20,000? Even with more, do you really want to spend $17,000 on a funeral? A few do, yes. And for that, we funeral directors are extremely grateful. But for those of you who don't, let's keep reading.

Exhibit B:

Option 1, Cost Reduction

Appendix – Exhibit B: Option 1, Cost Reduction

A Services

Professional Services

Basic Services of Funeral Director & Staff	$1,795.00
Embalming	$595.00
Other Preparation of Body	$200.00

Facilities

Use of Facilities for Viewing/Visitation	
Use of Facilities for Funeral Ceremony	$500.00
Use of Facilities for Memorial Service	
Use of Equipment & Staff for Graveside Service	
Use of Equipment & Staff for Church Service	

Transportation

Transfer of Remains to Funeral Home	$225.00
Hearse	$200.00
Limousine	
Sedan/Lead Car	$185.00
Service/Utility Vehicle	
	$3,700.00

B Merchandise

Casket (or Other Receptacle)		$3620.00
Name	A 58 Primrose	
Material	18-Gauge Steel	
Color	Pink Velvet Int.	

Outer Burial Container		$1,750.00
Name	Venetian	
Material	Concrete/Liner	
Flowers		$200.00

174

Appendix – Exhibit B: Option 1, Cost Reduction

Acknowledgement Cards	inc.
Register Book	$150.00
Memory Folders	inc.
Clothing	
Cremation Urn	
	$5720.00

C Special Charges

Cash Advances

Death Certificates	$36.00
Clergy	$125.00
Musician	$100.00
Paid Obituaries	$250.00
Vault Co. Fee	$325.00
Tax	$449.00
Total	**$1,285.00**

TOTAL	**$10,705.00**

This example of the" Statement of Goods and Services" shows a dramatic reduction in the total price; from $17,399 to $10,705...a difference of $6,694. What we've done here is declined two options from the service charge: The evening visitation and the limousine. As advocated earlier in the book, most visiting hours can be accomplished the same day as the funeral. Therefore the "Use of Facilities for Viewing/Visitation" will be removed. This allowed us to save $500. Also, removing the limousine saved another $200. So instead of $4,400 for the service charge, we are down to $3,700.

But if you **really** want to reduce the funeral price, always re-examine your choice of merchandise. Instead of the "Primrose Bronze", we've selected the A 58 White Rose, an almost identical casket, but made of 18-gauge steel, and some $3600 less. The vault chosen was the Venetian. Although this vault does not have the bronze liner of the previous selection, it is a protective vault which seals and will completely protect the casket from outside elements. Oh, I forgot, it's also $1,870 cheaper (oops, I mean "less expensive". "Cheaper" is such a negative word.) The Venetian is a beautiful vault with a marbelon liner and a carapace. As stated earlier in the book, if you want to impress anyone at the grave, this vault will undoubtedly do so. But remember, "impressing" is is not our goal here, especially if you're trying to save a few bucks.

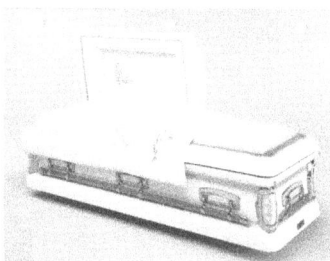

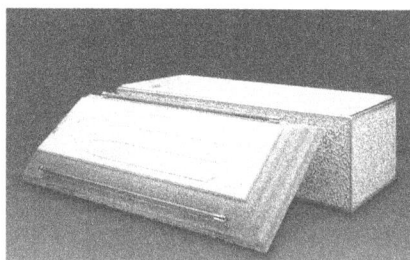

We've also reduced the money spent on flowers by $100, which will still allow you to have a beautiful family piece. These simple, yet unnoticable changes in your merchandise selections also saved us an additional $420 in sales tax.

Cash advances are a little tougher to change, but we did edit the obituary in the newspaper. Just leaving out the names of the grandkids, work history and her membership organizations saved us $300.00.

Saving $6,700 on a funeral is terrific, but we can do better. Follow me.....

Exhibit C:

Option 2, Cost Reduction

A Services

Professional Services

Basic Services of Funeral Director & Staff	$1,795.00
Embalming	$595.00
Other Preparation of Body	$200.00

Facilities

Use of Facilities for Viewing/Visitation	
Use of Facilities for Funeral Ceremony	$500.00
Use of Facilities for Memorial Service	
Use of Equipment & Staff for Graveside Service	
Use of Equipment & Staff for Church Service	

Transportation

Transfer of Remains to Funeral Home	$225.00
Hearse	$200.00
Limousine	
Sedan/Lead Car	$185.00
Service/Utility Vehicle	
	$3,700.00

B Merchandise

Casket (or Other Receptacle)		$2,046.00
	Name	Q 88 Primrose
	Material	20-Gauge Steel
	Color	Pink Crepe Interior

Outer Burial Container		$1,295.00
	Name	Monticello
	Material	Concrete/Liner
Flowers		$150.00
Acknowledgement Cards		inc.

Appendix – Exhibit C: Option 2, Cost Reduction

Register Book	$150.00
Memory Folders	inc.
Clothing	
Cremation Urn	
	$3,641.00

C Special Charges

Cash Advances

Death Certificates	$36.00
Clergy	$125.00
Musician	$100.00
Paid Obituaries	$250.00
Vault Co. Fee	$325.00
Tax	$286.00
Total	**$1,122.00**

TOTAL	**$8,463.00**

Our third review of the original "Statement of Goods & Services" saves us another $2,242. Once again we eliminated the evening visitation and limousine, which saved us $700. And again, we changed our casket selection from the A 58 White Rose, an 18-gauge steel casket to the Q 83 Primrose, a 20-gauge steel casket with the same feminine theme. Our vault selection was changed from the Venetian to the Monticello (my favorite vault). We also cut back on the flowers by $50. We'll still get a beautiful casket spray for $150. These simple yet cost-effective changes also saved us $163 in sales tax.

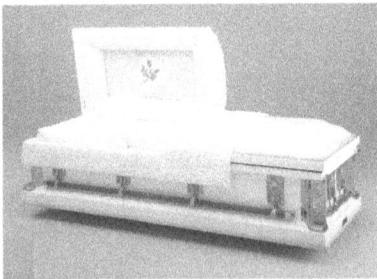

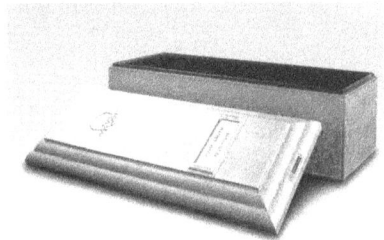

Earlier in the book I expressed my beliefs about how much protection a deceased human body needs while buried. Of course it's a personal decision, but I reminded you that the body will decompose from within a sealed casket because of anaerobic bacteria. Also, the casket will be exposed to moisture even if protected with a lined and sealed vault, because of the body's natural loss of fluids.

But what's interesting in this case, is there is still a great deal of "protection" from this merchandise. And remember, if you think the vault is too plain, it will be painted to match the casket and highlighted with gold or copper sparkles which will make for a beautiful presentation at the cemetery; dignified, yet much more reasonably priced.

So we started with a beautiful, high-priced funeral with a bronze casket and a double-lined vault to the tune of $17,399 and now we're down to $8,463, and we still have a beautiful casket, a matching, sealed vault, a lovely family flower spray for the casket, and professional and dignified

services…but we're not finished.

Notes

_____

_____

_____

_____

_____

_____

_____

_____

_____

_____

_____

Exhibit D:

Option 3, Cost Reduction

A Services

Professional Services

Basic Services of Funeral Director & Staff		$1,795.00
Embalming		
Other Preparation of Body		$200.00

Facilities

Use of Facilities for Viewing/Visitation		
Use of Facilities for Funeral Ceremony		$200.00
Use of Facilities for Memorial Service		
Use of Equipment & Staff for Graveside Service		
Use of Equipment & Staff for Church Service		

Transportation

Transfer of Remains to Funeral Home		$225.00
Hearse		$200.00
Limousine		
Sedan/Lead Car		
Service/Utility Vehicle		
		$2,620.00

B Merchandise

Casket (or Other Receptacle)		$1,600.00
Name	Ivory Pink	
Material	20-Gauge Steel	
Color	Pink Crepe Interior	

Outer Burial Container		$795.00
Name	Grave Liner	
Material	Concrete	
Flowers		$150.00

Acknowledgement Cards		inc.
Register Book		$150.00
Memory Folders		inc.
Clothing		
Cremation Urn		
		$2,695.00

C Special Charges

Cash Advances

Death Certificates	$36.00
Clergy	$125.00
Musician	$100.00
Paid Obituaries	$250.00
Vault Co. Fee	$260.00
Tax	$212.00
Total	**$983.00**

TOTAL	**$6298.00**

In our fourth look at this "traditional" service, we have taken even more steps to bring the cost down. First and foremost, we've chosen to decline certain options such as embalming and the sedan/lead car. Without embalming we will not have a public viewing, but we can still have a private viewing, perhaps for an hour at the funeral home immediately prior to the service. This saved us almost $600. The "Other Preparation of Body" still applies because the decedent was bathed, dressed, cosmetized and casketed.

The "Facilities" charge was brought down by $300 since the "Use Of" was decreased by several hours. Instead of a full visitation and service, we are opting for a private viewing and service not lasting for more than ninety minutes.

Since we've eliminated the sedan/lead car, we can ask the funeral director to lead the procession with the hearse. "What about the minister, Joe? Isn't he supposed to ride in the lead car?" The minister can ride in the hearse (the front seat). This just saved us $185.

Now let's take another look at the merchandise. Again, this is your biggest opportunity to save money. We have now selected a 20-gauge steel casket, only this time it's a "non-sealer". By now you know the difference between a sealer and a non-sealer and can make a clear choice as to what you want. This particular casket is called "Ivory Pink". It is simply a less expensive version of the three previous feminine themed caskets, only this one retails for $1,600 instead of $7,254 or $3,620 or $2,046.

Since the cemetery requires the casket be placed in some sort of "outer container", we've chosen the concrete grave liner instead of an actual vault. This saved us $500. The casket will not be in a "sealed" environment but it will be protected from the weight of the earth above it and the grave will not sink as badly.

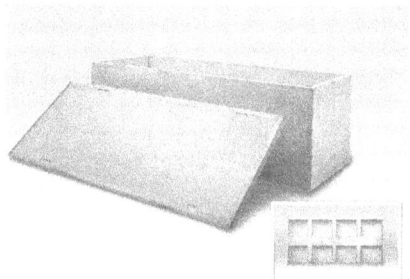

We've made one small change with the cash advances. We were able to save $65 from the "Vault Co. Fee" because we've opted to decline the tent and chairs. If the weather is good or there's a cemetery chapel, there would be no need to set up a tent and chairs for the committal service. This part of the service only lasts about ten minutes. A charge of $65 is a lot of money for ten minutes.

With these decisions, we were able to reduce the price of this funeral another $2,100, bringing the price down to $6,298, which **includes** $983 worth of cash advances and sales tax.

Notes

_____

_____

_____

_____

_____

_____

_____

_____

_____

_____

_____

Notes

_____

_____

_____

_____

_____

_____

_____

_____

_____

_____

_____

Notes

_____

_____

_____

_____

_____

_____

_____

_____

_____

_____

_____

_____

Notes

_____

_____

_____

_____

_____

_____

_____

_____

_____

_____

_____

About the Author

Joe Kalmer has been a licensed funeral director and embalmer for over 23 years. As a graduate of Worsham College of Mortuary Science, he received his formal funeral service education and training in what can only be described as a "baptism of fire". Learning the funeral industry in Chicago, his experience includes living in the basement of a west-side funeral home while working in the Cook County Morgue on a weekly basis.

He is the owner and founder of Kalmer Memorial services in O'Fallon IL, a non-traditional facility dedicated to offering consumers the choices not found in the traditional funeral homes where he first began his career. With unique and branded products such as his "cremation alliance" and "the discount funeral home", Joe is able to translate his dedication, professionalism and compassion to practical solutions that address the concerns of the average consumer.

With a variety of experiences to bring to the table, including past ownership of a very traditional funeral home in Edwardsville, Illinois, Joe demystifies the language and practices of the funeral industry as he meets the rising demand for cremation and "less traditional" forms of service. This provides an added benefit to his wife Cheryl — who welcomes the change in location from their living quarters above the funeral home with the master bedroom directly above the casketed remains in the chapel below.

Joe currently resides in Edwardsville, Illinois with his wife and two daughters.

www.ingramcontent.com/pod-product-compliance
Lightning Source LLC
Chambersburg PA
CBHW031251090426
42742CB00007B/408